Principles of politer knowing the v

Contributor: John Gregory, (Editor: John Trusler)

Alpha Editions

This edition published in 2024

ISBN 9789362515315

Design and Setting By
Alpha Editions
www.alphaedis.com
Email - info@alphaedis.com

As per information held with us this book is in Public Domain.
This book is a reproduction of an important historical work.
Alpha Editions uses the best technology to reproduce historical work
in the same manner it was first published to preserve its original nature.
Any marks or number seen are left intentionally to preserve.

Contents

INTRODUCTION	- 1 -
ADVERTISEMENT.	- 2 -
PRINCIPLES OF POLITENESS, &c.	- 3 -
MODESTY.	- 4 -
LYING.	- 7 -
GOOD-BREEDING.	- 9 -
GENTEEL CARRIAGE.	- 12 -
CLEANLINESS OF PERSON.	- 15 -
DRESS.	- 16 -
ELEGANCE OF EXPRESSION.	- 18 -
ADDRESS, PHRASEOLOGY, AND SMALL-TALK.	- 21 -
OBSERVATION.	- 23 -
ABSENCE OF MIND.	- 25 -
KNOWLEDGE OF THE WORLD.	- 27 -
CHOICE OF COMPANY.	- 34 -
LAUGHTER.	- 36 -
SUNDRY LITTLE ACCOMPLISHMENTS.	- 37 -
EMPLOYMENT OF TIME.	- 45 -
DIGNITY OF MANNERS.	- 47 -
RULES FOR CONVERSATION.	- 50 -
A FATHER'S LEGACY TO HIS DAUGHTERS.	- 57 -
RELIGION.	- 59 -
CONDUCT AND BEHAVIOUR.	- 63 -
AMUSEMENTS.	- 67 -

FRIENDSHIP, LOVE, MARRIAGE.

INTRODUCTION

TO THE PORTSMOUTH EDITION.

The two parts of this work, which have heretofore been printed separate, are now offered to the Public in one volume, as a system of polite and moral instruction for both sexes: This edition is critically corrected, with the special design of furnishing English schools, at a small expence, with a proper *book for reading and parsing their own language, that the teacher may be provided with suitable means for mending the manners of his pupils, while he informs their understandings, by analyzing the grammatical construction, and pointing out the beauties of the most approved style.*

PORTSMOUTH, *Jan. 1786.*

ADVERTISEMENT.

The late Lord CHESTERFIELD *having been universally allowed to be one of the best bred men of the age, and most intimately acquainted with the principles and manners of mankind, the Editor of the following pages humbly apprehends he could not do the rising generation a greater service, than by collecting those valuable precepts which are contained in his celebrated letters to his son, digesting them under distinct heads, and thereby forming a system of the most useful instruction.*

To that end, he has diligently selected every observation and remark that can possibly improve or inform the mind, within the rules of morality: and where there seemed a deficiency in any part of the system, from the occasional chasms in Lord Chesterfield's correspondence, he has endeavoured to supply it. Much might have been said on the subject of indelicacy, but as instructions on that head, to persons possessed of a liberal education, must have been unnecessary, they are here purposely omitted. Some may be apt to think, that many things in this work are too frivolous to be mentioned; but when it is remembered they are calculated for the multitude, it is presumed they will be received as respectable admonitions. In short, it has been the Editor's study to make Lord Chesterfield useful to every class of youth; to lay that instruction before them, which they with difficulty must have found amidst a heap of other matter; in a word, to give the very essence of his letters, and at a tenth part of the price *those letters sell for.*

PRINCIPLES OF POLITENESS, &c.

ADDRESSED TO
EVERY YOUNG GENTLEMAN.

As all young men, on their first outset in life, are in want of some experienced and friendly hand to bring them forward, and teach them a knowledge of the world; I think I cannot do the rising generation a greater service, than by directing the young man's steps, and teaching him how to make his way among the crowd. I will suppose him already instructed in the principles of religion, and necessity of moral virtues; (for without these he must be most unhappy) of course shall, in a series of chapters, point out, under distinct heads, the qualifications necessary to make him well received in the world; without which, he cannot expect to bear his part in life, agreeably to his own wishes, or the duty he owes to society; and as modesty is the basis of a proper reception, I shall begin with that.

MODESTY.

Modesty is a polite accomplishment, and generally an attendant upon merit: It is engaging to the highest degree, and wins the heart of all our acquaintance. On the contrary, none are more disgustful in company than the impudent and presuming.

THE man who is, on all occasions, commending and speaking well of himself, we naturally dislike. On the other hand, he who studies to conceal his own defects, who does justice to the merit of others, who talks but little of himself, and that with modesty, makes a favourable impression on the persons he is conversing with, captivates their minds, and gains their esteem.

MODESTY, however, widely differs from an awkward bashfulness, which is as much to be condemned as the other is to be applauded. To appear simple is as ill-bred as to be impudent. A young man ought to be able to come into a room and address the company, without the least embarrassment. To be out of countenance when spoken to, and not to have an answer ready, is ridiculous to the last degree.

AN awkward country fellow, when he comes into company better than himself, is exceedingly disconcerted. He knows not what to do with his hands, or his hat, but either puts one of them in his pocket, and dangles the other by his side; or perhaps twirls his hat on his fingers, or fumbles with the button. If spoken to, he is in a much worse situation, he answers with the utmost difficulty, and nearly stammers; whereas a gentleman, who is acquainted with life, enters a room with gracefulness and a modest assurance, addresses even persons he does not know, in an easy and natural manner, and without the least embarrassment. This is the characteristic of good-breeding, a very necessary knowledge in our intercourse with men; for one of inferior parts, with the behaviour of a gentleman, is frequently better received than a man of sense, with the address and manners of a clown.

IGNORANCE and vice are the only things we need be ashamed of; steer clear of these, and you may go into any company you will: Not that I would have a young man throw off all dread of appearing abroad; as a fear of offending, or being disesteemed, will make him observe a proper decorum. Some persons from experiencing the inconveniencies of false modesty, have run into the other extreme, and acquired the character of impudent: This is as great a fault as the other. A well-bred man keeps himself within the two, and steers the middle way. He is easy and firm in every company, is modest but not bashful, steady but not impudent. He copies the manners of the better people, and conforms to their customs with ease and attention.

TILL we can present ourselves in all companies with coolness and unconcern, we can never present ourselves well; nor will a man ever be supposed to have kept good company, or ever be acceptable in such company, if he cannot appear there easy and unembarrassed. A modest assurance, in every part of life, is the most advantageous qualification we can possibly acquire.

INSTEAD of becoming insolent, a man of sense, under a consciousness of merit, is more modest. He behaves himself indeed with firmness, but without the least presumption. The man who is ignorant of his own merit, is no less a fool than he who is constantly displaying it. A man of understanding avails himself of his abilities, but never boasts of them; whereas the timid and bashful can never push himself in life, be his merit as great as it will; he will be always kept behind by the forward and bustling. A man of abilities, and acquainted with life, will stand as firm in defence of his own rights, and pursue his plans as steadily and unmoved, as the most impudent man alive; but then he does it with a seeming modesty. Thus manner is every thing; what is impudence in one, is proper assurance only in another; for firmness is commendable, but an overbearing conduct is disgustful.

FORWARDNESS being the very reverse of modesty, follow rather than lead the company; that is, join in discourse upon subjects, rather than start one of your own: If you have parts, you will have opportunities enough of shewing them on every topic of conversation, and if you have none, it is better to expose yourself upon a subject of other people's than of your own.

BUT, be particularly careful not to speak of yourself, if you can help it. An impudent fellow lugs in himself abruptly upon all occasions, and is ever the hero of his own story. Others will colour their arrogance with, 'It may seem strange, indeed, that I should talk in this manner of myself; it is what I by no means like, and should never do, if I had not been cruelly and unjustly accused; but when my character is attacked, it is a justice I owe to myself, to defend it.' This veil is too thin not to be seen through on the first inspection.

OTHERS again, with more art, will *modestly* boast of all the principal virtues, by calling those virtues weaknesses, and saying, they are so unfortunate as to fall into weaknesses. 'I cannot see persons suffer,' says one of this cast, 'without relieving them; though my circumstances are very unable to afford it.' 'I cannot avoid speaking truth, though it is often very imprudent,' and so on.

THIS angling for praise is so prevailing a principle, that it frequently stoops to the lowest objects. Men will often boast of doing that, which, if true, would be rather a disgrace to them than otherwise. One man affirms that he rode twenty miles within the hour; 'tis probably a lie; but suppose he did, what then? He had a good horse under him, and is a good jockey. Another swears he has often at a sitting, drank five or six bottles to his own share. Out of respect to him, I will believe *him* a liar, for I would not wish to think him a beast.

THESE and many more are the follies of idle people, which, while they think they procure them esteem, in reality make them despised.

TO avoid this contempt, therefore, never speak of yourself at all, unless necessity obliges you; and even then, take care to do it in such a manner, that it may not be construed in to fishing for applause. Whatever perfections you may have, be assured, people will find them out; but whether they do or not, nobody will take them upon your own word. The less you say of yourself, the more the world will give you credit for; and the more you say, the less they will believe you.

LYING.

OF all the vices, there is no one more criminal, more mean, and more ridiculous, than lying. The end we design by it is very seldom accomplished, for lies are always found out, at one time or other; and yet there are persons who give way to this vice, who are otherwise of good principles, and have not been ill educated.

LIES generally proceed from vanity, cowardice, and a revengeful disposition, and sometimes from a mistaken notion of self-defence.

HE who tells a malicious lie, with a view of injuring the person he speaks of, may gratify his wish for a while, but will, in the end, find it recoil upon himself; for, as soon as he is detected (and detected he most certainly will be) he is despised for the infamous attempt, and whatever he may say hereafter of that person, will be considered as false, whether it be so or not.

IF a man lies, shuffles, or equivocates, for, in fact, they are all alike, by way of excuse for any thing he has said or done, he aggravates the offence rather than lessens it; for the person to whom the lie is told has a right to know the truth, or there would have been no occasion to have framed a falsehood. This person, of course, will think himself ill treated for being a second time affronted; for what can be a greater affront than an attempt to impose upon any man's understanding? Besides, lying, in excuse for a fault, betrays fear, than which nothing is more dastardly, and unbecoming the character of a gentleman.

THERE is nothing more manly, or more noble, if we have done wrong, than frankly to own it. It is the only way of meeting forgiveness. Indeed, confessing a fault and asking pardon, with great minds, is considered as a sufficient atonement. 'I have been betrayed into an error,' or 'I have injured you, Sir, and am heartily ashamed of it, and sorry for it,' has frequently disarmed the person injured, and where he would have been our enemy, has made him our friend.

THERE are persons also, whose *vanity* leads them to tell a thousand lies. They persuade themselves, that if it be no way injurious to others, it is harmless and innocent, and they shelter their falsehoods under the softer name of *untruths*. These persons are foolish enough to imagine, that if they can recite any thing wonderful, they draw the attention of the company, and if they themselves are the objects of that wonder, they are looked up to as persons extraordinary. This has made many men to see things that never were in being, hear things that never were said, atchieve feats that never were attempted, dealing always in the marvellous. Such may be assured, however unwilling the persons they are conversing with may be to laugh in their faces, that they hold them secretly in the highest contempt; for he who will tell a lie thus idly, will not scruple to tell a greater, where his interest is concerned. Rather than any person should doubt of my veracity for one minute, I would deprive myself of telling abroad either what I had really seen or heard, if such things did not carry with them the face of probability.

OTHERS again will boast of the great respect they meet with in certain companies; of the honors that are continually heaped on them there; of the great price they give for every thing they purchase; and this to be thought of consequence; but, unless such people have the best and most accurate memory, they will, perhaps, very soon after, contradict their former assertions, and subject themselves to contempt and derision.

REMEMBER then as long as you live, that nothing but strict truth can carry you through life with honor and credit. Liars are not only disagreeable but dangerous companions, and, when known, will ever be shunned by men of understanding. Besides, as the greatest liars are generally the greatest fools, a man who addicts himself to this detestable vice, will not only be looked upon as vulgar, but will never be considered as a man of sense.

GOOD-BREEDING.

VOID of good-breeding, every other qualification will be imperfect, unadorned, and to a certain degree unavailing.

GOOD-BREEDING being the result of good sense and good nature, is it not wonderful that people possessed of the one, should be deficient in the other? The modes of it, varying according to persons, places, and circumstances, cannot indeed be acquired otherwise than by time and observation, but the substance is every where and always the same.

WHAT good morals are to society in general, good manners are to particular ones; their band and security. Of all actions, next to that of performing a good one, the consciousness of rendering a civility is the most grateful.

WE seldom see a person, let him be ever so ill-bred, want in respect to those whom he acknowledges to be his superiors; the manner of shewing this respect, then, is all I contend for. The well-bred man expresses it naturally and easily, while he who is unused to good company expresses it awkwardly. Study, then, to shew that respect which every one wishes to shew, in an easy and grateful way; but this must be learnt by observation.

IN company with your equals, or in mixed companies, a greater latitude may be taken in your behaviour; yet, it should never exceed the bounds of decency; for, though no one in this case, can claim any distinguished marks of respect, every one is entitled to civility and good manners. A man need not, for example, fear to put his hands in his pockets, take snuff, sit, stand, or occasionally walk about the room; but it would be highly unbecoming to whistle, wear his hat, loosen his garters, or throw himself across the chairs. Such liberties are offensive to our equals, and insulting to our inferiors. Easiness of carriage by no means implies inattention and carelessness. No one is at liberty to act, in all respects, as he pleases; but is bound by the laws of good manners to behave with decorum.

LET a man talk to you ever so stupidly or frivolously, not to pay some attention to what he says, is savageness to the greatest degree. Nay, if he even forces his conversation to you, it is worse than rudeness not to listen to him; for your inattention in this case, tells him, in express terms, that you think him a blockhead and not worth the hearing. Now, if such behaviour is rude to men, it is much more so to women, who, be their rank what it will, have, on account of their sex, a claim to officious attention from the men. Their little wants and whims, their likes and dislikes, and even their impertinences, are particularly attended to and flattered, and their very thoughts and wishes guessed at and instantly gratified, by every well-bred man.

IN promiscuous companies, you should vary your address, agreeably to the different ages of the persons you speak to. It would be rude and absurd to talk of your amours or your pleasures to men of certain dignity and gravity, to clergymen, or men in years; but still you should be as easy with them as with others, your manner only should be varied; you should, if possible, double your respect and attention to them; and were you to insinuate occasionally, that from their observation and experience you wish to profit, you would insensibly win their esteem; for flattery, if not fulsome and gross, is agreeable to all.

WHEN invited to dinner or supper, you must never usurp to yourself the best places, the best dishes, &c. but always decline them, and offer them to others, except, indeed, you are offered any thing by a superior, when it would be a rudeness, if you liked it, not to accept it immediately, without the least apology.—Thus, for example, was a superior, the master of the table, to offer you a thing of which there was but one, to pass it to the person next you, would be indirectly charging him that offered it to you, with a want of good manners and proper respect to his company; or, if you were the only stranger present, it would be a rudeness if you make a feint of refusing it with the customary apology, 'I cannot think of taking it from you, sir;' or, 'I am sorry to deprive you of it;' as it is supposed he is conscious of his own rank, and if he chose not to give it, would not have offered it; your apology therefore, in this case, is putting him upon an equality with yourself. In like manner, it is rudeness to draw back when requested by a superior to pass a door first, or to step into a carriage before him. In short, it would be endless to particularise all the instances in which a well-bred man shews his politeness in good company, such as not yawning, singing, whistling, warming his breech at the fire, lounging, putting his legs upon the chairs, and the like, familiarities every man's good sense must condemn, and good-breeding abhor.

BUT, good-breeding consists in more than merely not being ill-bred. To return a bow, speak when you are spoken to, and say nothing rude, are such negative acts of good-breeding, that they are little more than not being a brute. Would it not be a very poor commendation of any man's cleanliness, to say that he was not offensive? If we wish for the good will and esteem of our acquaintance, our good-breeding must be active, cheerful, officious and seducing.

FOR example, should you invite any one to dine or sup with you, recollect whether ever you had observed them to prefer one thing to another, and endeavour to procure that thing; when at table, say, 'At such a time, I think you seemed to give this dish a preference, I therefore ordered it.' 'This is the wine I observed you like best, I have therefore been at some pains to procure it.' Trifling as these things may appear, they prove an attention to the person they are said to; and as attention in trifles is the test of respect, the compliment will not be lost.

I NEED only refer you to your own breast. How have these little attentions, when shewn you by others, flattered that self-love which no man is free from? They incline and attach us to that person, and prejudice us afterwards, to all that he says or does. The declaration of the women in a great degree stamps a man's reputation of being either ill or well-bred; you must then, in a manner, overwhelm them with these attentions; they are used to them, and naturally expect them, and to do them justice, they are seldom lost upon them. You must be sedulous to wait upon them, pick up with alacrity any thing they drop, and be very officious in procuring their carriages or their chairs in public places; be blind to what you should not see, and deaf to what you should not hear. Opportunities of shewing these attentions are continually presenting themselves; but in case they should not, you must study to create them.

IF ever you would be esteemed by the women, your conversation to them should be always respectful, lively, and addressed to their vanity. Every thing you say or do, should tend to shew a regard to their beauty or good sense: Even men are not without their vanities of one kind or another, and flattering that vanity by words and looks of approbation, is one of the principal characters of good-breeding.

ADDRESS and manners, with weak persons, who are actually three-fourths of the world, are every thing; and even people of the best understanding are taken in with them. Where the heart is not won, and the eye pleased, the mind will be seldom on our side.

IN short, learning and erudition, without good-breeding, are tiresome and pedantic; and an ill-bred man is as unfit for good company, as he will be unwelcome in it. Nay, he is full as unfit for business as for company. Make, then, good-breeding the great object of your thoughts and actions. Be particularly observant of, and endeavour to imitate, the behaviour and manners of such as are distinguished by their politeness; and be persuaded, that good-breeding is to all worldly qualifications, what charity is to all Christian virtues; it adorns merit, and often covers the want of it.

GENTEEL CARRIAGE.

NEXT to good-breeding is a genteel manner and carriage, wholly free from those ill habits and awkward actions, which many very worthy persons are addicted to.

A GENTEEL manner of behaviour, how trifling so-ever it may seem, is of the utmost consequence in private life. Men of very inferior parts have been esteemed, merely for their genteel carriage and good-breeding, while sensible men have given disgust for want of it. There is something or other that prepossesses us at first sight, in favour of a well-bred man, and makes us wish to like him.

WHEN an awkward fellow first comes into a room, he attempts to bow, and his sword, if he wears one, goes between his legs, and nearly throws him down. Confused and ashamed, he stumbles to the upper end of the room, and seats himself in the very chair he should not. He there begins playing with his hat, which he presently drops; and recovering his hat, he lets fall his cane; and in picking up his cane, down goes his hat again; thus 'tis a considerable time before he is adjusted. When his tea or coffee is handed to him, he spreads his handkerchief upon his knees, scalds his mouth, drops either the cup or the saucer, and spills the tea or coffee in his lap. At dinner he is more uncommonly awkward; there he tucks his napkin through a button-hole, which tickles his chin, and occasions him to make a variety of wry faces; he seats himself upon the edge of the chair, at so great a distance from the table, that he frequently drops his meat between his plate and his mouth; he holds his knife, fork and spoon differently from other people; eats with his knife, to the manifest danger of his mouth; picks his teeth with his fork, rakes his mouth with his finger, and puts his spoon which has been in his throat a dozen times, into the dish again. If he is to carve, he cannot hit the joint, but in labouring to cut through the bone, splashes the sauce over every body's cloaths. He generally daubs himself all over, his elbows are in the next person's plate, and he is up to the knuckles in soup and grease. If he drinks, it is with his mouth full, interrupting the whole company with 'To your good health, sir,' and 'My service to you;' perhaps coughs in his glass, and be-sprinkles the whole table. Further, he has perhaps a number of disagreeable tricks, he snuffs up his nose, picks it with his fingers, blows it, and looks in his handkerchief, crams his hands first into his bosom, and next into his breeches. In short, he neither dresses nor acts like any other person, but is particularly awkward in every thing he does. All this, I own, has nothing in it criminal; but it is such an offence to good manners and good-breeding, that it is universally despised; it makes a man ridiculous in every company, and, of course, ought carefully to be avoided by every one who would wish to please.

FROM this picture of the ill-bred man, you will easily discover that of the well-bred; for you may readily judge what you ought to do, when you are told what you ought not to do; a little attention to the manners of those who have seen the world, will make a proper behaviour habitual and familiar to you.

ACTIONS, that would otherwise be pleasing, frequently become ridiculous by the manner of doing them. If a lady drop her fan in company, the worst-bred man would immediately pick it up, and give it to her; the best bred man can do no more; but then he does it in a graceful manner, that is sure to please; whereas the other would do it so awkwardly as to be laughed at.

YOU may also know a well-bred person by his manner of sitting. Ashamed and confused, the awkward man sits in his chair stiff and bolt upright, whereas the man of fashion, is easy in every position; instead of lolling or lounging as he sits, he leans with elegance, and by varying his attitudes, shews that he has been used to good company. Let it be one part of your study then, to learn to sit genteely in different companies, to loll gracefully, where you are authorized to take that liberty, and sit up respectfully, where that freedom is not allowable.

IN short, you cannot conceive how advantageous a graceful carriage and a pleasing address are, upon all occasions; they ensnare the affections, seal a prepossession in our favour, and play about the heart till they engage it.

NOW to acquire a graceful air, you must attend to your dancing; no one can either sit, stand or walk well, unless he dances well. And, in learning to dance, be particularly attentive to the motion of your arms, for a stiffness in the wrist will make any man look awkward. If a man walks well, presents himself well in company, wears his hat well, moves his head properly, and his arms gracefully, it is almost all that is necessary.

THERE is also an awkwardness in speech, that naturally falls under this head, and ought to and may be guarded against; such as forgetting names, and mistaking one name for another; to speak of Mr. What-d'ye-call-him, or You-know-who, Mrs. Thingum, What's-her-name, or How-d'ye-call-her, is exceedingly awkward and vulgar. It is the same to address people by improper titles, as *sir* for *my lord*; to begin a story without being able to finish it, and break off in the middle, with, 'I have forgot the rest.'

OUR voice and manner of speaking too, should likewise be attended to. Some will mumble over their words, so as not to be intelligible, and others will speak so fast as not to be understood, and, in doing this, will spatter and spit in your face; some will bawl as if they were speaking to the deaf;

others will speak so low as scarcely to be heard; and many will put their face so close to yours, as to offend you with their breath. All these habits are horrid and disgustful, but may easily be got the better of, with care. They are the vulgar characteristics of a low-bred man, or are proofs that very little pains have been bestowed in his education. In short, an attention to these little matters is of greater importance than you are aware of; many sensible men having lost ground for want of these little graces, and many, possessed of these perfections alone, having made their way through life, who otherwise would not have been noticed.

CLEANLINESS OF PERSON.

BUT, as no one can please in company, however graceful in his air, unless he be clean and neat in his person, this qualification comes next to be considered.

NEGLIGENCE of one's person not only implies an unsufferable indolence, but an indifference whether we please or not. It betrays an insolence and affectation, arising from a presumption, that we are sure of pleasing, without having recourse to those means which many are obliged to use.

HE who is not thoroughly clean in his person, will be offensive to all he converses with. A particular regard to the cleanliness of your mouth, teeth, hands and nails, is but common decency. A foul mouth and unclean hands, are certain marks of vulgarity; the first is the cause of an offensive breath, which nobody can bear, and the last is declarative of dirty work; one may always know a gentleman by the state of his hands and nails. The flesh at the roots should be kept back, so as to shew the semicircles at the bottom of the nails; the edges of the nails should never be cut down below the ends of the fingers, nor should they be suffered to grow longer than the fingers. When the nails are cut down to the quick, it is a shrewd sign that the man is a mechanic, to whom long nails would be troublesome, or that he gets his bread by fiddling; and if they are longer than his fingers' ends, and encircled with a black rim, it foretells he has been laboriously and meanly employed, and too fatigued to clean himself; a good apology for want of cleanliness in a mechanic, but the greatest disgrace that can attend a gentleman.

THESE things may appear too insignificant to be mentioned; but when it is considered that a thousand little nameless things, which every one feels, but no one can describe, conspire to form that *whole* of pleasing, I hope you will not call them trifling. Besides, a clean shirt and a clean person are as necessary to health, as not to offend other people. It is a maxim with me, which I have lived to see verified, that he who is negligent at twenty years of age, will be a sloven at forty, and intolerable at fifty.

DRESS.

NEATNESS of person, I observed, was as necessary as cleanliness; of course, some attention must be paid to your dress.

SUCH is the absurdity of the times, that to pass well with the world, we must adopt some of its customs, be they ridiculous or not.

IN the first place, to neglect one's dress is to affront all the female part of our acquaintance. The women in particular pay an attention to their dress; to neglect therefore yours will displease them, as it would be tacitly taxing them with vanity, and declaring that you thought them not worth that respect which every body else does. And, as I have mentioned before, it being the women who stamp a young man's credit in the fashionable world, if you do not make yourself agreeable to them, you will assuredly lose ground among the men.

DRESS, as trifling as it may appear to a man of understanding, prepossesses on the first appearance, which is frequently decisive. And indeed we form some opinion of a man's sense and character from his dress. Any exceeding of the fashion, or any affectation whatever in dress, argues a weakness in understanding, and nine times in ten, it will be found so.

THERE are few young fellows but what display some character or other in this shape. Some would be thought fearless and brave; these wear a black cravat, a short coat and waistcoat, an uncommon long sword hanging to their knees, a large hat fiercely cocked, and are *flash* all over. Others affect to be country squires; these will go about in buckskin breeches, brown frocks, and great oaken cudgels in their hands, slouched hats, with their hair undressed and tucked up under them to an enormous size, and imitate grooms and country boobies so well externally, that there is not the least doubt of their resembling them as well internally. Others, again, paint and powder themselves so much, and dress so finically, as leads us to suppose they are only women in boy's cloaths. Now a sensible man carefully avoids all this, or any other affectation. He dresses as fashionably and as well as persons of the best families and best sense; if he exceeds them, he is a coxcomb; if he dresses worse, he is unpardonable.

DRESS yourself fine, then, if possible, or plain, agreeably to the company you are in; that is, conform to the dress of others, and avoid the appearance of being tumbled. Imitate those reasonable people of your own age, whose dress is neither remarked as too neglected or too much studied. Take care to have your clothes well made, in the fashion, and to fit you, or you will, after all, appear awkward. When once dressed, think no more of it; shew no fear of discomposing your dress, but let all your motions be as easy and unembarrassed, as if you were at home in your dishabille.

ELEGANCE OF EXPRESSION.

HAVING mentioned elegance of person, I will proceed to elegance of expression.

IT is not one or two qualifications alone complete the gentleman; it must be a union of many; and graceful speaking is as essential as gracefulness of person. Every man cannot be a harmonious speaker; a roughness or coarseness of voice may prevent it; but if there are no natural imperfections, if a man does not stammer or lisp, or has not lost his teeth, he may speak gracefully; nor will all these defects, if he has a mind to it, prevent him from speaking correctly.

NOBODY can attend with pleasure to a bad speaker. One who tells his story ill, be it ever so important, will tire even the most patient. If you have been present at the performance of a good tragedy, you have doubtless been sensible of the good effects of a speech well delivered; how much it has interested and affected you; and on the contrary, how much an ill spoken one has disgusted you. 'Tis the same in common conversation; he who speaks deliberately, distinctly and correctly: He who makes use of the best words to express himself, and varies his voice according to the nature of the subject, will always please, while the thick or hasty speaker, he who mumbles out a set of ill-chosen words, utters them ingrammatically, or with a dull monotony, will tire and disgust. Be assured then, the air, the gesture, the looks of a speaker, a proper accent, a just emphasis, and tuneful cadence, are full as necessary to please and be attended to, as the subject matter itself.

PEOPLE may talk what they will of solid reasoning and sound sense; without the graces and ornaments of language, they will neither please nor persuade. In common discourse, even trifles elegantly expressed will be better received than the best of arguments homespun and unadorned.

A GOOD way to acquire a graceful utterance is to read aloud to some friend every day, and beg of him to set you right, in case you read too fast, do not observe the proper stops, lay a wrong emphasis, or utter your words indistinctly. You may even read aloud to yourself, where such a friend is not at hand, and you will find your own ear a good corrector. Take care to open your teeth when you read or speak, and articulate every word distinctly; which last cannot be done, but by sounding the final letter. But above all, endeavour to vary your voice, according to the matter, and avoid a monotony. By a daily attention to this, it will, in a little time, become easy and habitual to you.

PAY an attention also to your looks and your gestures, when talking even on the most trifling subjects; things appear very different according as they are expressed, looked and delivered.

NOW, if it is necessary to attend so particularly to our *manner* of speaking, it is much more so, with respect to the *matter*. Fine turns of expression, a genteel and correct style, are ornaments as requisite to common sense, as polite behaviour and an elegant address are to common good manners; they are great assistants in the point of pleasing. A gentleman, 'tis true, may be known in the meanest garb, but it admits not of a doubt, that he would be better received into good company, genteelly and fashionably dressed, than if he appeared in dirt and tatters.

BE careful then of your style upon all occasions; whether you write or speak, study for the best words and best expressions, even in common conversation, or the most familiar letters. This will prevent your speaking in a hurry, than which nothing is more vulgar; though you may be a little embarrassed at first, time and use will render it easy. It is no such difficult thing to express ourselves well on subjects we are thoroughly acquainted with, if we think before we speak; and no one should presume to do otherwise. When you have said a thing, if you did not reflect before, be sure to do it afterwards; consider with yourself, whether you could not have expressed yourself better; and if you are in doubt of the propriety or elegancy of any word, search for it in some dictionary,[1] or some good author, while you remember it: Never be sparing of your trouble while you would wish to improve, and my word for it, a very little time will make this matter habitual.

> 1. Johnson's folio Dictionary *you will find very serviceable*; and the Difference between Words reputed synonimous; *a work in two volumes, written by me some years ago, and published by Dodsley.*

IN order to speak grammatically, and to express yourself pleasingly, I would recommend it to you to translate often any language you are acquainted with into English, and to correct such translation till the words, their order, and the periods, are agreeable to your own ear.

VULGARISM in language is another distinguishing mark of bad company and education. Expressions may be correct in themselves, and yet be vulgar, owing to their not being fashionable; for language and manners are both established by the usage of people of fashion.

THE conversation of a low-bred man is filled up with proverbs and hackneyed sayings. Instead of observing that tastes are different, and that most men have one peculiar to themselves, he will give you, 'What is one man's meat is another man's poison;' or, 'Every one to their liking, as the old woman said, when she killed her cow.' He has ever some favourite word, which he lugs in upon all occasions, right or wrong; such as *vastly* angry, *vastly* kind; *devilish* ugly, *devilish* handsome; *immensely* great, *immensely* little. Even his pronunciation carries the mark of vulgarity along with it; he calls the earth, *yearth*; finan'ces, *fin'ances*; he goes *to words*, and not towards such a place. He affects to use hard words, to give him the appearance of a man of learning, but frequently mistakes their meaning, and seldom, if ever, pronounces them properly.

ALL this must be avoided, if you would not be supposed to have kept company with footmen and housemaids. Never have recourse to proverbial or vulgar sayings; use neither favourite nor hard words, but seek for the most elegant; be careful in the management of them, and depend on it your labour will not be lost; for nothing is more engaging than a fashionable and polite address.

ADDRESS, PHRASEOLOGY, AND SMALL-TALK.

IN all good company, we meet with a certain manner, phraseology, and general conversation, that distinguish the man of fashion. These can only be acquired by frequenting good company, and being particularly attentive to all that passes there.

WHEN invited to dine or sup at the house of any well-bred man, observe how he does the honors of his table, and mark his manner of treating his company.

ATTEND to the compliments of congratulation or condolence that he pays; and take notice of his address to his superiors, his equals and his inferiors; nay, his very looks and tone of voice, are worth your attention, for we cannot please without a union of them all.

THERE is a certain distinguishing diction that marks the man of fashion, a certain language of conversation that every gentleman should be master of. Saying to a man just married, 'I wish you joy,' or to one who has lost his wife, 'I am sorry for your loss,' and both perhaps with an unmeaning countenance, may be civil, but it is nevertheless vulgar. A man of fashion will express the same thing more elegantly, and with a look of sincerity, that shall attract the esteem of the person he speaks to. He will advance to the one, with warmth and cheerfulness, and perhaps squeezing him by the hand, will say, 'Believe me, my dear Sir, I have scarce words to express the joy I feel, upon your happy alliance with such or such a family,' &c. To the other in affliction, he will advance slower, and with a peculiar composure of voice and countenance, begin his compliments of condolence with, 'I hope, Sir, you will do me the justice to be persuaded, that I am not insensible of your unhappiness, that I take part in your distress, and shall ever be affected where *you* are so.'

YOUR first address to, and indeed all your conversation with, your superiors, should be open, cheerful and respectful; with your equals warm and animated; with your inferiors, hearty, free and unreserved.

THERE is a fashionable kind of small-talk, which however trifling it may be thought, has its use in mixed companies: Of course you should endeavour to acquire it. By small-talk, I mean a good deal to say on unimportant matters; for example, foods, the flavour and growth of wines, and the chit-chat of the day. Such conversation will serve to keep off serious subjects, that might sometimes create disputes. This chit-chat is chiefly to be learned by frequenting the company of the ladies.

OBSERVATION.

AS the art of pleasing is to be learnt only by frequenting the best companies, we must endeavor to pick it up in such companies by observation; for, it is not sense and knowledge alone that will acquire esteem; these certainly are the first and necessary foundations for pleasing, but they will by no means do, unless attended with manners and attentions.

THERE have been people who have frequented the first companies all their life time, and yet have never got rid of their natural stiffness and awkwardness; but have continued as vulgar as if they were never out of a servant's hall: This has been owing to carelessness, and a want of attention to the manners and behaviour of others.

THERE are a great many people likewise who busy themselves the whole day, and who in fact do nothing. They have possibly taken up a book for two or three hours, but from a certain inattention that grows upon them the more it is indulged, know no more of the contents than if they had not looked into it; nay, it is impossible for any one to retain what he reads, unless he reflects and reasons upon it as he goes on. When they have thus lounged away an hour or two, they will saunter into company, without attending to any thing that passes there; but, if they think at all, are thinking of some trifling matter that ought not to occupy their attention; thence perhaps they go to the play, where they stare at the company and the lights, without attending to the piece, the very thing they went to see. In this manner they wear away their hours, that might otherwise be employed to their improvement and advantage. This silly suspension of thought they would pass for *absence of mind*—ridiculous!—Wherever you are, let me recommend it to you to pay an attention to all that passes; observe the characters of the persons you are with, and the subjects of their conversation; listen to every thing that is said, see every thing that is done, and (according to the vulgar saying) have your eyes and your ears about you.

A CONTINUAL inattention to matters that occur, is the characteristic of a weak mind; the man who gives way to it, is little else than a trifler, a blank in society, which every sensible person overlooks; surely what is worth doing, is worth doing well, and nothing can be well done, if not properly attended to. When I hear a man say, on being asked about any thing that was said or done in his presence, 'that truly he did not mind it.' I am ready to knock the fool down. *Why* did not he mind it?—What else had he to do?—A man of sense and fashion never makes use of this paltry plea, he never complains of a treacherous memory, but attends to and remembers every thing that is either said or done.

WHENEVER, then, you go into good company, that is the company of people of fashion, observe carefully their behaviour, their address and their manner; imitate them as far as in your power. Your attention, if possible, should be so ready as to observe every person in the room at once, their motions, their looks, and their turns of expression, and that without staring, or seeming to be an observer. This kind of observation may be acquired by care and practice, and will be found of the utmost advantage to you, in the course of life.

ABSENCE OF MIND.

HAVING mentioned absence of mind, let me be more particular concerning it.

WHAT the world calls an absent man, is generally either a very affected one, or a very weak one; but whether weak or affected, he is, in company, a very disagreeable man. Lost in thought, or possibly in no thought at all, he is a stranger to every one present, and to every thing that passes; he knows not his best friends, is deficient in every act of good manners, unobservant of the actions of the company, and insensible to his own. His answers are quite the reverse of what they ought to be; talk to him of one thing, he replies, as of another. He forgets what he said last, leaves his hat in one room, his cane in another, and his sword in a third; nay, if it was not for his buckles, he would even leave his shoes behind him. Neither his arms nor his legs seem to be a part of his body, and his head is never in a right position. He joins not in the general conversation, except it be by fits and starts, as if awaking from a dream: I attribute this either to weakness or affectation. His shallow mind is possibly not able to attend to more than one thing at a time; or he would be supposed wrap'd up in the investigation of some very important matter. Such men as Sir Isaac Newton or Mr. Locke, might occasionally have some excuse for absence of mind! It might proceed from that intenseness of thought which was necessary at all times for the scientific subjects they were studying; but, for a young man, and a man of the world, who has no such plea to make, absence of mind is rudeness to the company, and deserves the severest censure.

HOWEVER insignificant a company may be; however trifling their conversation; while you are with them, do not shew them, by an inattention, that you think them trifling; that can never be the way to please, but rather fall in with their weakness than otherwise; for to mortify, or shew the least contempt to those we are in company with, is the greatest rudeness we can be guilty of, and what few can forgive.

I NEVER yet found a man inattentive to the person he feared, or the woman he loved; which convinces me, that absence of mind is to be got the better of, if we think proper to make the trial; and believe me, it is always worth the attempt.

ABSENCE of mind is a tacit declaration, that those we are in company with, are not worth attending to; and what can be a greater affront?——Besides, can an absent man improve by what is said or done in his presence? No; he may frequent the best companies for years together, and all to no purpose.

In short, a man is neither fit for business nor conversation, unless he can attend to the object before him, be that object what it will.

KNOWLEDGE OF THE WORLD.

A KNOWLEDGE of the world, by our own experience and observation, is so necessary, that, without it, we shall act very absurdly, and frequently give offence, when we do not mean it. All the learning and parts in the world, will not secure us from it. Without an acquaintance with life, a man may say very good things, but time them so ill, and address them so improperly, that he had much better be silent. Full of himself, and his own business, and inattentive to the circumstances and situations of those he converses with, he vents it without the least discretion, says things that he ought not to say, confuses some, shocks others, and puts the whole company in pain, lest what he utters next should prove worse than the last. The best direction I can give you in this matter, is rather to fall in with the conversation of others, than start a subject of your own; rather strive to put them more in conceit with themselves, than to draw their attention to you.

A NOVICE in life, he who knows little of mankind, but what he collects from books, lays it down as a maxim, that most men love flattery; in order therefore to please, he will flatter. But how? Without regard either to circumstances or occasion. Instead of those delicate touches, those soft tints, that serve to heighten the piece, he lays on his colours with a heavy hand, and daubs, where he means to adorn; in other words, he will flatter so unseasonably, and at the same time so grossly, that while he wishes to please, he puts out of countenance, and is sure to offend. On the contrary, a man of the world, one who has made life his study, knows the power of flattery as well as he; but, then, he knows how to apply it; he watches the opportunity, and does it indirectly, by inference, comparison and hint.

MAN is made up of such a variety of matter, that to search him thoroughly, requires time and attention; for, though we are all made of the same materials, and have all the same passions, yet, from a difference in their proportion and combination, we vary in our dispositions; what is agreeable to one is disagreeable to another, and what one shall approve, another shall condemn. Reason is given us to controul these passions, but seldom does it. Application therefore to the reason of any man, will frequently prove ineffectual, unless we endeavour at the same time to gain his heart.

WHEREVER then you are, search into the characters of men; find out if possible, their foible, their governing passion, or their particular merit; take them on their weak side, and you will generally succeed; their prevailing vanity you may readily discover, by observing their favourite topic of conversation; for every one talks most, of what he would be thought most to excel in.

THE time should also be judiciously made choice of. Every man has his particular times, when he may be applied to with success, the *mollia tempora fandi*; but these times are not all day long, they must be found out, watched, and taken advantage of. You could not hope for success in applying to a man about one business, when he was taken up with another, or when his mind was affected with excess of grief, anger, or the like.

YOU cannot judge of other men's minds better than by studying your own; for though one man has one foible, and another has another, yet men, in general, are very much alike. Whatever pleases or offends you, will, in similar circumstances, please or offend others; if you find yourself hurt, when another makes you feel his superiority, you will certainly upon the common rule of right, *Do as you would be done by*, take care not to let another feel *your* superiority, if you have it; especially if you wish to gain his interest or esteem. If disagreeable insinuations, open contradictions, or oblique sneers, vex and anger you, would you use them where you wished to please? Certainly not. Observe then, with care, the operations of your own mind, and you may, in a great measure, read all mankind.

I WILL allow that one bred up in a cloister or college, may reason well on the structure of the human mind; he may investigate the nature of man, and give a tolerable account of his head, his heart, his passions, and his sentiments: but at the same time he may know nothing of him; he has not lived with him, and of course knows but little how those sentiments or those passions will work.—He must be ignorant of the various prejudices, propensities and antipathies, that always bias him, and frequently determine him. His knowledge is acquired only from theory, which differs widely from practice; and if he forms his judgment from that alone, he must be often deceived; whereas a man of the world, one who collects his knowledge from his own experience and observation, is seldom wrong; he is well acquainted with the operations of the human mind; prys into the heart of man; reads his words, before they are uttered; sees his actions, before they are performed; knows what will please and what will displease, and foresees the event of most things.

LABOUR then to acquire this intuitive knowledge; attend carefully to the address, the arts and manners of those acquainted with life, and endeavour to imitate them. Observe the means they take, to gain the favour, and conciliate the affections of those they associate with; pursue those means, and you will soon gain the esteem of all that know you.

HOW often have we seen men governed by persons very much their inferiors in point of understanding, and even without their knowing it? A proof that some men have more worldly dexterity than others; they find out the weak and unguarded part, make their attack there, and the man surrenders.

NOW from a knowledge of mankind we shall learn the advantage of two things, the command of our temper and countenances; a trifling, disagreeable incident shall perhaps anger one unacquainted with life, or confound him with shame; shall make him rave like a madman, or look like a fool; but a man of the world will never understand what he cannot or ought not to resent. If he should chance to make a slip himself, he will stifle his confusion, and turn it off with a jest, recovering it with coolness.

MANY people have sense enough to keep their own secrets; but from being unused to a variety of company, have unfortunately such a tell-tale countenance, as involuntarily declares what they would wish to conceal. This is a great unhappiness, and should, as soon as possible, be got the better of.

THAT coolness of mind, and evenness of countenance, which prevent a discovery of our sentiments, by our words, our actions, or our looks, are too necessary to pass unnoticed. A man who cannot hear displeasing things, without visible marks of anger or uneasiness; or pleasing ones, without a sudden burst of joy, a cheerful eye, or an expanded face, is at the mercy of every knave; for either they will designedly please or provoke you themselves, to catch your unguarded looks; or they will seize the opportunity thus to read your very heart, when another shall do it. You may possibly tell me, that this coolness must be natural, for if not, you can never acquire it. I will admit the force of constitution, but people are very apt to blame *that*, for many things they might readily avoid. Care, with a little reflection, will soon give you this mastery of your temper and countenance. If you find yourself subject to sudden starts of passion, determine with yourself not to utter a single word till your reason has recovered itself; and resolve to keep your countenance as unmoved as possible. As a man, who at a card table can preserve a serenity in his looks, under good or bad luck, has considerably the advantage of one who appears elated with success, or cast down with ill fortune, from our being able to read his cards in his face, so the man of the world, having to deal with one of these babbling countenances, will take care to profit by the circumstance, let the consequence, to him with whom he deals, be as injurious as it may.

IN the course of life, we shall find it necessary very often to put on a pleasing countenance, when we are exceedingly displeased; we must frequently seem friendly, when we are quite otherwise. I am sensible it is difficult to accost a man with smiles whom we know to be our enemy; but what is to be done? On receiving an affront, if you cannot be justified in knocking the offender down, you must not notice the offence; for, in the eye of the world, taking an affront calmly is considered as cowardice.

IF fools should attempt at any time to be witty upon you, the best way is not to know their witticisms are leveled at you, and to conceal any uneasiness it may give you; but, should they be so plain that you cannot be thought ignorant of their meaning, I would recommend, rather than quarrel with the company, joining even in the laugh against yourself; allowing the jest to be a good one, and take it in seeming good humour. Never attempt to retaliate the same way, as that would imply you were hurt. Should what is said wound your honor, or your moral character, there is but one proper reply, which I hope you will never be obliged to have recourse to.

REMEMBER there are but two alternatives for a gentleman; extreme politeness, or the sword. If a man openly and designedly affronts you, call him out; but, if it does not amount to an open insult, be outwardly civil; if this does not make him ashamed of his behaviour, it will prejudice every by-stander in your favour, and instead of being disgraced, you will come off with honor. Politeness to those we do not respect, is no more a breach of faith, than *your humble servant* at the bottom of a challenge; they are universally understood to be things of course.

WRANGLING and quarrelling characterize a weak mind; leave them to those who love such conduct, be *you* always above it. Enter into no sharp contest, and pride yourself, in shewing, if possible, more civility to your antagonist than to any other in the company; this will infallibly bring over all the laughers to your side, and the person you are contending with, will be very likely to confess you have behaved very handsomely throughout the whole affair.

EXPERIENCE will teach us, that though all men consist principally of the same materials, as I before took notice of, yet from a difference in their proportion, no two men are uniformly the same; we differ from one another, and we often differ from ourselves, that is, we sometimes do things utterly inconsistent with the general tenor of our characters. The wisest man may occasionally do a weak thing; the most honest man, a wrong thing; the proudest man, a mean thing; and the worst of men will sometimes do a good thing. On this account, our study of mankind should not be general; we should take a frequent view of individuals, and though we may upon the whole, form a judgment of the man from his prevailing passion or his general character, yet it will be prudent not to determine, till we have waited to see the operations of his subordinate appetites and humours.

FOR example; a man's general character may be that of strictly honest. I would not dispute it, because, I would not be thought envious or malevolent; but I would not rely upon this general character, so as to entrust him with my fortune or my life. Should this honest man, as is not uncommon, be my rival in power, interest, or love, he may possibly do things that in other circumstances he would abhor; and power, interest, and love, let me tell you, will often put honesty to the severest trial, and frequently overpower it. I would then ransack this honest man to the bottom, if I wished to trust him, and as I found him, would place my confidence accordingly.

ONE of the great compositions in our nature is vanity; to which all men, more or less, give way. Women have an intolerable share of it. No flattery, no adulation, is too gross for many of them; those who flatter them most, please them best; and they are most in love with him who pretends to be most in love with them; and the least slight or contempt of them is seldom forgotten. It is, in some measure, the same with men; they will sooner pardon an injury than an insult, and are more hurt by contempt than by ill usage. Though all men do not boast of superior talents, though they pretend not to the abilities of a Pope, a Newton, or a Bolingbroke, every one pretends to have common sense, and to discharge his office in life with common decency; to arraign, therefore, in any shape, his abilities or integrity, in the department he holds, is an insult he will not readily forgive.

AS I would not have you trust too implicitly to a man, because the world gives him a good character, so I must particularly caution you against those who speak well of themselves. In general, suspect those who boast of or affect to have any one virtue above all others, for they are commonly impostors. There are exceptions however to this rule; for we hear of prudes that have been chaste, bullies that have been brave, and saints that have been religious. Confide only where your own observation shall direct you; observe not only what is said, but how it is said, and if you have any penetration, you may find out the truth better by your eyes than your ears; in short, never take a character upon common report, but enquire into it yourself; for common report, though it is right in general, may be wrong in particulars.

BEWARE of those who, on a slight acquaintance, make you a tender of their friendship, and seem to place a confidence in you; it is ten to one but they deceive and betray you; however, do not rudely reject them upon such a supposition; you may be civil to them, though you do not entrust them. Silly men are apt to solicit your friendship, and unbosom themselves upon the first acquaintance; such friends cannot be worth having, their friendship being as slender as their understanding; and if they proffer their friendship with a design to make a property of you, they are dangerous acquaintance indeed. Not but the little friendships of the weak may be of some use to you, if you do not return the compliment; and it may not be amiss to seem to accept of those designing men, keeping them, as it were, in play, that they may not be openly your enemies; for their enmity is the next dangerous thing to their friendship. We may certainly hold their vices in abhorrence, without being marked out as their personal enemy. The general rule is, to have a real reserve with almost every one, and a seeming reserve with almost no one; for it is very disgusting to seem reserved, and very dangerous not to be so. Few observe the true medium. Many are ridiculously mysterious upon trifles, and many indiscreetly communicative of all they know.

THERE is a kind of short-lived friendship that takes place among young men, from a connexion in their pleasures only; a friendship too often attended with bad consequences. This companion of your pleasures, young and unexperienced, will probably, in the heat of convivial mirth, vow a perpetual friendship, and unfold himself to you without the least reserve; but new associations, change of fortune, or change of place, may soon break this ill-timed connexion, and an improper use may be made of it. Be one, if you will, in young companies, and bear your part like others, in all the social festivity of youth; nay, trust them with your innocent frolicks, but keep your serious matters to yourself; and if you must at any time make *them* known, let it be to some tried friend of great experience; and that nothing may tempt him to become your rival, let that friend be in a different walk of life from yourself.

WERE I to hear a man making strong protestations and swearing to the truth of a thing, that is in itself probable and very likely to be, I should doubt his veracity; for when he takes such pains to make me believe it, it cannot be with a good design.

THERE is a certain easiness or false modesty in most young people, that either makes them unwilling, or ashamed to refuse any thing that is asked of them. There is also an unguarded openness about them, that makes them the ready prey of the artful and designing. They are easily led away by the feigned friendships of a knave or a fool, and too rashly place a confidence in them, that terminates in their loss, and frequently in their ruin. Beware, therefore, as I said before, of these proffered friendships; repay them with compliments, but not with confidence. Never let your vanity make you suppose that people become your friends upon a slight acquaintance; for good offices must be shewn on both sides to create a friendship: It will not thrive, unless its love be mutual; and it requires time to ripen it.

THERE is still among young people another kind of friendship merely nominal; warm indeed for the time, but fortunately of no long continuance. This friendship takes its rise from their pursuing the same course of riot and debauchery; their purses are open to each other, they tell one another all they know, they embark in the same quarrels, and stand by each other on all occasions. I should rather call this a confederacy against good morals and good manners, and think it deserves the severest lash of the law; but they have the impudence to call it friendship. However, it is often as suddenly dissolved as it is hastily contracted; some accident disperses them, and they presently forget each other, except it is to betray, and to laugh at their own egregious folly.

IN short, the sum of the whole is, to make a wide difference between companions and friends; for a very agreeable companion has often proved a very dangerous friend.

CHOICE OF COMPANY.

THE next thing to the choice of friends, is the choice of your company.

ENDEAVOUR, as much as you can, to keep good company, and the company of your superiors; for you will be held in estimation according to the company you keep. By superiors, I do not mean so much with regard to birth, as merit, and the light in which they are considered by the world.

THERE are two sorts of good company, the one consists of persons of birth, rank, and fashion; the other, of those who are distinguished by some particular merit, in any liberal art or science, as men of letters, &c. and a mixture of these is what I would have understood by good company: For it is not what particular sets of people shall call themselves, but what the people in general acknowledge to be so, and are the accredited good company of the place.

NOW and then, persons without either birth, rank, or character, will creep into good company, under the protection of some considerable personage; but, in general, none are admitted of mean degree, or infamous moral character.

IN this fashionable good company alone, can you learn the best manners and the best language; for, as there is no legal standard to form them by, it is here they are established.

IT may possibly be questioned, whether a man has it always in his power to get into good company; undoubtedly, by deserving it, he has, provided he is in circumstances which enable him to live and appear in the stile of a gentleman. Knowledge, modesty, and good-breeding, will endear him to all that see him; for without politeness, the scholar is no better than a pedant, the philosopher than a cynic, the soldier than a brute, nor any man than a clown.

THOUGH the company of men of learning and genius is highly to be valued and occasionally coveted, I would by no means have you always found in such company. As they do not live in the world, they cannot have that easy manner and address, which I would wish you to acquire. If you can bear a part in such company, it is certainly advisable to be in it sometimes, and you will be the more esteemed in other company by being so; but let it not engross you, lest you should be considered as one of the *literati*, which however respectable in name, is not the way to rise or shine in the fashionable world.

BUT the company which, of all others, you should carefully avoid, is that, which, in every sense of the word may be called *low*; low in birth, low in rank, low in parts, and low in manners; that company, who, insignificant and contemptible in themselves, think it an honor to be seen with *you*, and who will flatter your follies, nay your very vices, to keep you with them.

THOUGH *you* may think such a caution unnecessary, I do not; for many a young gentleman of sense and rank, has been led by his vanity to keep such company, till he has been degraded, vilified and undone.

THE vanity I mean, is that of being the first of the company. This pride, though too common, is idle to the last degree. Nothing in the world lets a man down so much. For the sake of dictating, being applauded and admired by this low company, he is disgraced and disqualified for better. Depend upon it, in the estimation of mankind, you will sink or rise to the level of the company you keep.

BE it, then, your ambition to get into the best company; and, when there, imitate their virtues, but not their vices. You have, no doubt, often heard of genteel and fashionable vices. These are whoring, drinking and gaming. It has happened that some men, even with these vices, have been admired and esteemed. Understand this matter rightly, it is not their vices for which they are admired; but for some accomplishments they at the same time possess; for their parts, their learning, or their good-breeding. Be assured, were they free from their vices, they would be much more esteemed. In these mixed characters, the bad part is overlooked for the sake of the good.

SHOULD you be unfortunate enough to have any vices of your own, add not to their number, by adopting the vices of others. Vices of adoption are of all others the most unpardonable; for they have not inadvertency to plead. If people had no vices but their own, few would have so many as they have.

IMITATE, then, only the perfections you meet with; copy the politeness, the address, the easy manners of well-bred people; and remember, let them shine ever so bright, if they have any vices, they are so many blemishes, which it would be as ridiculous to imitate, as it would, to make an artificial wart upon one's face, because some very handsome man had the misfortune to have a natural one upon his.

LAUGHTER.

LET us now descend to minute matters, which, though not so important as those we mentioned, are still far from inconsiderable. Of these laughter is one.

FREQUENT and loud laughter is a sure sign of a weak mind, and no less characteristic of a low education. It is the manner in which low-bred men express their silly joy, at silly things, and they call it being merry.

I DO not recommend upon all occasions a solemn countenance. A man may smile, but if he would be thought a gentleman and a man of sense, he would by no means laugh. True wit never made a man of fashion laugh; he is above it. It may create a smile, but as loud laughter shews, that a man has not the command of himself, every one, who would wish to appear sensible, must abhor it.

A MAN'S going to sit down, on a supposition that he has a chair behind him, and falling for want of one, occasions a general laugh, when the best pieces of wit would not do it; a sufficient proof how low and unbecoming laughter is.

BESIDES, could the immoderate laugher hear his own noise, or see the faces he makes, he would despise himself for his folly. Laughter being generally supposed to be the effects of gaiety, its absurdity is not properly attended to; but a little reflection will easily restrain it; and when you are told, it is a mark of low-breeding, I persuade myself you will endeavour to avoid it.

SOME people have a silly trick of laughing, whenever they speak; so that they are always on the grin, and their faces ever distorted. This and a thousand other tricks, such as scratching their heads, twirling their hats, fumbling with their button, playing with their fingers, &c. &c. are acquired from a false modesty, at their first outset in life. Being shame-faced in company, they try a variety of ways to keep themselves in countenance; thus, they fall into those awkward habits I have mentioned, which grow upon them, and in time become habitual.

NOTHING is more repugnant likewise to good-breeding than horse play of any sort, romping, throwing things at one another's heads, and so on. They may pass well enough with the mob, but they lessen and degrade the gentleman.

SUNDRY LITTLE ACCOMPLISHMENTS.

I HAVE had reason to observe before, that various little matters, apparently trifling in themselves, conspire to form the *whole* of pleasing, as, in a well finished portrait, a variety of colours combine to compleat the piece. It not being necessary to dwell much upon them, I shall content myself, with just mentioning them as they occur.

1. TO do the honors of a table gracefully, is one of the outlines of a well-bred man; and to carve well, is an article, little as it may seem, that is useful twice every day, and the doing of which ill, is not only troublesome to one's self, but renders us disagreeable and ridiculous to others. We are always in pain for a man, who instead of cutting up a fowl genteely, is hacking for half an hour across the bone, greasing himself, and bespattering the company with the sauce. Use, with a little attention, is all that is requisite to acquit yourself well in this particular.

2. TO be well received, you must, also, pay some attention to your behaviour at table, where it is exceedingly rude to scratch any part of your body, to spit, or blow your nose, if you can possibly avoid it, to eat greedily, to lean your elbows on the table, to pick your teeth before the dishes are removed, or to leave the table before grace is said.

3. DRINKING of healths is now growing out of fashion, and is very unpolite in good company. Custom had once made it universal, but the improved manners of the age now render it vulgar. What can be more rude or ridiculous than to interrupt persons at their meals, with an unnecessary compliment? Abstain then from this silly custom, where you find it out of use; and use it only at those tables where it continues general.

4. "A POLITE" manner of refusing to comply with the solicitations of a company, is also very necessary to be learnt; for, a young man, who seems to have no will of his own, but does every thing that is asked of him, may be a very good natured fellow, but he is a very silly one. If you are invited to drink at any man's house, more than you think is wholesome, you may say, 'you wish you could, but that so little makes you both drunk and sick, that you should only be bad company by doing it; of course beg to be excused.' If desired to play at cards deeper than you would, refuse it ludicrously; tell them, 'if you were sure to lose, you might possibly sit down; but that, as fortune may be favourable, you dread the thought of having too much money, ever since you found what an incumbrance it was to poor Harlequin, and therefore you are resolved never to put yourself in the way of winning more than such or such a sum a day.' This light way of declining

invitations, to vice and folly, is more becoming a young man than philosophical or sententious refusals, which would only be laughed at.

5. NOW I am on the subject of cards, I must not omit mentioning the necessity of playing them well and genteely, if you would be thought to have kept good company. I would by no means recommend playing of cards as a part of your study, lest you should grow too fond of it, and the consequences prove bad. It were better not to know a diamond from a club, than to become a gambler; but as custom has introduced innocent card-playing at most friendly meetings, it marks the gentleman to handle them genteely, and play them well; and as I hope you will play only for small sums, should you lose your money, pray lose it with temper; or win, receive your winnings without either elation or greediness.

6. TO write well and correct, and in a pleasing stile, is another part of polite education. Every man who has the use of his eyes and his right hand, can write whatever hand he pleases. Nothing is so illiberal as a school-boy's scrawl. I would not have you learn a stiff formal hand-writing, like that of a schoolmaster, but a genteel, legible and liberal hand, and to be able to write quick. As to the correctness and elegancy of your writing, attention to grammar does the one, and to the best authors, the other. Epistolary correspondence should not be carried on in a studied or affected style, but the language should flow from the pen, as naturally and as easily as it would from the mouth. In short, a letter should be penned in the same style, as you would talk to your friend, if he were present.

7. IF writing well shews the gentleman, much more so does spelling well. It is essentially necessary for a gentleman, or a man of letters; one false spelling may fix a ridicule on him for the remainder of his life. Words in books are generally well spelled, according to the orthography of the age; reading therefore, with attention, will teach every one to spell right. It sometimes happens that words are spelled differently by different authors; but if you spell them upon the authority of one, in estimation of the public, you will escape ridicule. Where there is but one way of spelling a word, by your spelling it wrong, you will be sure to be laughed at. For a *woman* of a tolerable education would laugh at and despise her lover, if he wrote to her, and the words were ill spelled. Be particularly attentive then to your spelling.

8. THERE is nothing that a young man, at his first appearance in life, ought more to dread, than having any ridicule fixed on him. In the estimation even of the most rational men, it will lessen him, but ruin him with all the rest. Many have been undone by a ridiculous nick-name. The causes of nick-names among well-bred men, are generally the little defects in manner, air, or address. To have the appellation of ill-bred, awkward, muttering, left-

legged, or any other, tacked always to your name, would injure you more than you are aware of. Avoid then these little defects (and they are easily avoided) and you need never fear a nick-name.

9. SOME young men are apt to think, that they cannot be complete gentlemen, without becoming men of pleasure; and the rake they often mistake for the man of pleasure. A rake is made up of the meanest and most disgraceful vices. They all combine to degrade his character, and ruin his health and fortune. A man of pleasure will refine upon the enjoyments of the age, attend them with decency, and partake of them becomingly. Indeed, he is too often less scrupulous than he should be, and frequently has cause to repent it. A man of pleasure, at best, is but a dissipated being, and what the rational part of mankind must abhor; I mention it, however, lest in taking up the man of pleasure, you should fall into the rake; for of two evils, always chuse the least. A dissolute, flagitious footman may make as good a rake as a man of the first quality. Few men can be men of pleasure; every man may be a rake. There is a certain dignity that should be preserved in all our pleasures: In love, a man may lose his heart, without losing his nose; at table, a man may have a distinguishing palate, without being a glutton; he may love wine, without being a drunkard; he may game, without being a gambler; and so on. Every virtue has its kindred vice, and every pleasure its neighbouring disgrace. Temperance and moderation mark the gentleman; but excess the blackguard. Attend carefully, then, to the line that divides them; and remember, stop rather a yard short, than step an inch beyond it. Weigh the present enjoyment of your pleasures against the necessary consequences of them, and I will leave you to your own determination.

10. A GENTLEMAN has ever some regard also to the *choice* of his amusements; if at cards, he will not be seen at cribbage, all-fours, or put; or, in sports of exercise, at skittles, foot-ball, leap-frog, cricket, driving of coaches, &c. but will preserve a propriety in every part of his conduct; knowing that any imitation of the manners of the mob, will unavoidably stamp him with vulgarity. There is another amusement too, which I cannot help calling illiberal, that is, playing upon any musical instrument. Music is commonly reckoned one of the liberal arts, and undoubtedly is so; but to be piping or fiddling at a concert is degrading to a man of fashion. If you love music, hear it; pay fiddlers to play to you, but never fiddle yourself. It makes a gentleman appear frivolous and contemptible, leads him frequently into bad company, and wastes that time which might otherwise be well employed.

11. SECRECY is another characteristic of good-breeding. Be careful never to tell in one company what you see or hear in another; much less to divert the present company at the expense of the last. Things apparently

indifferent may, when often repeated and told abroad, have much more serious consequences than imagined. In conversation, there is generally a tacit reliance, that what is said will not be repeated; and a man, though not enjoined to secrecy, will be excluded company, if found to be a tatler; besides, he will draw himself into a thousand scrapes, and every one will be afraid to speak before him.

12. PULLING out your watch in company unasked, either at home or abroad, is a mark of ill-breeding; if at home, it appears as if you were tired of your company, and wished them to be gone; if abroad, as if the hours dragged heavily, and wished to be gone yourself. If you want to know the time, withdraw; besides, as the taking what is called French leave was introduced, that on one person's leaving the company the rest might not be disturbed, looking at your watch does what that piece of politeness was designed to prevent; it is a kind of dictating to all present, and telling them it is time, or almost time to break up.

13. AMONG other things, let me caution you against ever being in a hurry; a man of sense may be in haste, but he is never in a hurry; convinced that hurry is the surest way to make him do what he undertakes ill. To be in a hurry is a proof that the business we embark in is too great for us; of course it is the mark of little minds, that are puzzled and perplexed, when they should be cool and deliberate; they want to do every thing at once, and therefore do nothing. Be steady, then, in all your engagements; look round you, before you begin; and remember that you had better do half of them well, and leave the rest undone, than to do the whole indifferently.

14. FROM a kind of false modesty, most young men are apt to consider familiarity as unbecoming. Forwardness I allow is so; but there is a decent familiarity that is necessary in the course of life. Mere formal visits, upon formal invitations, are not the thing; they create no connexion, nor will they prove of service to you; it is the careless and easy ingress and egress, at all hours, that secures an acquaintance to our interest; and this is acquired by a respectful familiarity entered into, without forfeiting your consequence.

15. IN acquiring new acquaintance, be careful not to neglect your old, for a slight of this kind is seldom forgiven. If you cannot be with your former acquaintance, so often as you used to be, while you had no others, take care not to give them cause to think you neglect them; call upon them frequently, though you cannot stay long with them; tell them you are sorry to leave them so soon, and nothing should take you away but certain engagements which good manners oblige you to attend to; for it will be your interest to make all the friends you can, and as few enemies as possible. By friends, I would not be understood to mean confidential ones; but persons who speak of you respectfully, and who, consistent with their

own interest, would wish to be of service to you, and would rather do you good than harm.

16. ANOTHER thing I must recommend to you, as characteristic of a polite education, and of having kept good company, is a graceful manner of conferring favours. The most obliging things may be done so awkwardly as to offend, while the most disagreeable things may be done so agreeably as to please.

17. A FEW more articles and then I have done; the first is on the subject of vanity. It is the common failing of youth, and as such ought to be carefully guarded against. The vanity I mean, is that which, if given way to, stamps a man a coxcomb, a character he will find a difficulty to get rid of, perhaps as long as he lives. Now this vanity shews itself in a variety of shapes; one man shall pride himself in taking the lead in all conversations, and peremptorily deciding upon every subject; another, desirous of appearing successful among the women, shall insinuate the encouragement he has met with, the conquests he makes, and perhaps boasts of favours he never received; if he speaks truth, he is ungenerous; if false, he is a villain; but whether true or false, he defeats his own purposes, overthrows the reputation he wishes to erect, and draws upon himself contempt in the room of respect. Some men are vain enough to think they acquire consequence by alliance, or by an acquaintance with persons of distinguished character or abilities; hence they are eternally talking of their grand-father, Lord such-a-one; their kinsman, Sir William such-a-one; or their intimate friend, Dr. such-a-one, with whom perhaps, they are scarcely acquainted. If they are ever found out (and that they are sure to be one time or another) they become ridiculous and contemptible; but even admitting what they say to be true, what then? A man's intrinsic merit does not rise from an ennobled alliance, or a reputable acquaintance. A rich man never borrows. When angling for praise, modesty is the surest bait. If we would wish to shine in any particular character, we must never affect that character. An affectation of courage will make a man pass for a bully; an affectation of wit, for a coxcomb; and an affectation of sense, for a fool. Not that I would recommend bashfulness or timidity: No; I would have every one know his own value, yet not discover that he knows it, but leave his merit to be found out by others.

18. ANOTHER thing worth your attention is, if in company with an inferior, not to let him feel his inferiority; if he discovers it himself, without your endeavours, the fault is not yours, and he will not blame you; but if you take pains to mortify him, or to make him feel himself inferior to you in abilities, fortune, or rank, it is an insult that will not readily be forgiven. In point of abilities, it would be unjust, as they are out of his power; in point of rank or fortune, it is ill-natured and ill-bred. This rule is never more necessary than at table, where there cannot be a greater insult than to help

an inferior to a part he dislikes, or a part that may be worse than ordinary, and to take the best to yourself. If you at any time invite an inferior to your table, you put him, during the time he is there, upon an equality with you; and it is an act of the highest rudeness to treat him in any respect, slightingly. I would rather double my attention to such a person, and treat him with additional respect, lest he should even suppose himself neglected. There cannot be a greater savageness, or cruelty, or any thing more degrading to a man of fashion than to put upon or take unbecoming liberties with him, whose modesty, humility, or respect, will not suffer him to retaliate. True politeness consists in making every body happy about you; and as to mortify is to render unhappy, it can be nothing but the worst of breeding. Make it a rule, rather to flatter a person's vanity than otherwise; make him, if possible, more in love with himself, and you will be certain to gain his esteem; never tell him any thing he may not like to hear, nor say things that will put him out of countenance, but let it be your study on all occasions to please; this will be making friends instead of enemies, and be a mean of serving yourself in the end.

19. NEVER be witty, at the expense of any one present, nor gratify that idle inclination which is too strong in most young men, I mean laughing at, or ridiculing the weaknesses or infirmities of others, by way of diverting the company, or displaying your own superiority. Most people have their weaknesses, their peculiar likings and aversions. Some cannot bear the sight of a cat; others the smell of cheese, and so on; were you to laugh at these men for their antipathies, or by design or inattention to bring them in their way, you could not insult them more. You may possibly thus gain the laugh on your side, for the present, but it will make the person, perhaps, at whose expense you are merry, your enemy forever after; and even those who laugh with you, will on a little reflection, fear you and probably despise you; whereas, to procure what *one* likes, and to remove what the *other* hates, would shew them that they were the objects of your attention, and possibly make them more your friends than much greater services would have done. If you have wit, use it to please but not to hurt. You may shine, but take care not to scorch. In short, never seem to see the faults of others. Though among the mass of men there are, doubtless, numbers of fools and knaves, yet were we to tell every one we meet with, that we know them to be so, we should be in perpetual war. I would detest the knave and pity the fool, wherever I found him, but I would let neither of them know unnecessarily that I did so; as I would not be industrious to make myself enemies. As one must please others then, in order to be pleased one's self, consider what is agreeable to you, must be agreeable to them, and conduct yourself accordingly.

20. WHISPERING in company is another act of ill-breeding: It seems to insinuate either that the persons who we would not wish should hear, are unworthy of our confidence, or it may lead them to suppose we are speaking improperly of them; on both accounts, therefore, abstain from it.

21. SO pulling out one letter after another and reading them in company, or cutting and paring one's nails, is unpolite and rude. It seems to say, we are weary of the conversation, and are in want of some amusement to pass away the time.

22. HUMMING a tune to ourselves, drumming with our fingers on the table, making a noise with our feet, and such like, are all breaches of good manners, and indications of our contempt for the persons present; therefore they should not be indulged.

23. WALKING fast in the streets is a mark of vulgarity, implying hurry of business; it may appear well in a mechanic or tradesman, but suits ill with the character of a gentleman, or a man of fashion.

24. STARING at any person you meet full in the face, is an act also of ill-breeding; it looks as if you saw something wonderful in his appearance, and is therefore a tacit reprehension.

25. EATING quick, or very slow at meals, is characteristic of the vulgar; the first infers poverty, that you have not had a good meal for some time; the last, if abroad, that you dislike your entertainment; if at home, that you are rude enough to set before your friends what you cannot eat yourself. So again, eating your soup with your nose in the plate is vulgar; it has the appearance of being used to hard work, and of course an unsteady hand. If it be necessary then to avoid this, it is much more so that of smelling your meat.

26. SMELLING to the meat while on the fork, before you put it in your mouth. I have seen many an ill-bred fellow do this, and have been so angry, that I could have kicked him from the table. If you dislike what you have upon your plate, leave it; but on no account, by smelling to, or examining it, charge your friend with putting unwholesome provisions before you.

27. SPITTING on the carpet is a nasty practice, and shocking, in a man of liberal education. Were this to become general, it would be as necessary to change the carpets as the table-cloths; besides, it will lead our acquaintance to suppose, that we have not been used to genteel furniture; for this reason alone, if for no other, by all means avoid it.

28. KEEP yourself free likewise from odd tricks or habits, such as thrusting out your tongue continually, snapping your fingers, rubbing your hands, sighing aloud, an affected shivering of your whole body, gaping with a noise

like a country-fellow that has been sleeping in a hay-loft, or indeed with any noise, and many others, which I have noticed before; these are imitations of the manners of the mob, and are degrading to a gentleman.

A VERY little attention will get the better of all these ill-bred habits, and be assured, you will find your account in it.

EMPLOYMENT OF TIME.

EMPLOYMENT of time, is a subject, that from its importance, deserves your best attention. Most young gentlemen have a great deal of time before them, and one hour well employed, in the early part of life, is more valuable and will be of greater use to you, than perhaps four and twenty, some years to come.

WHATEVER time you can steal from company, and from the study of the world; (I say company, for a knowledge of life is best learned in various companies) employ it in serious reading. Take up some valuable book, and continue the reading of that book, till you have got through it; never burden your mind with more than one thing at a time: And in reading this book don't run over it superficially, but read every passage twice over, at least do not pass on to a second till you thoroughly understand the first, nor quit the book till you are master of the subject; for unless you do this, you may read it through, and not remember the contents of it for a week. The books I would particularly recommend, among others, are, *Cardinal Retz's Maxims*, *Rochfaucault's Moral Reflections*, *Bruyere's Characters*, *Fontenell's Plurality of Worlds*, *Sir Josiah Child on Trade*, *Bolingbroke's Works*; for style, his *Remarks on the History of England*, under the name of Sir John Oldcastle; *Puffendorf's Jus Gentium*, and *Grotius' de Jure Belli et Pacis*. The last two are well translated by Barboyrac. For occasional half-hours or less, read the best works of invention, wit and humour; but never waste your minutes on trifling authors, either ancient or modern.

ANY business you may have to transact, should be done the first opportunity, and finished, if possible without interruption; for by deferring it, we may probably finish it too late, or execute it indifferently. Now, business of any kind should never be done by halves, but every part of it should be well attended to: For he that does business ill, had better not do it at all. And, in any point, which discretion bids you pursue, and which has a manifest utility to recommend it, let no difficulties deter you; rather let them animate your industry. If one method fails, try a second and a third. Be active, persevere and you will certainly conquer.

NEVER indulge a lazy disposition; there are few things but are attended with some difficulties, and if you are frightened at those difficulties, you will not compleat any thing. Indolent minds prefer ignorance to trouble; they look upon most things as impossible, because perhaps they are difficult. Even an hour's attention is too laborious for them, and they would rather content themselves with the first view of things, than take the trouble to look any farther into them. Thus, when they come to talk upon subjects to those who have studied them, they betray an unpardonable ignorance, and lay themselves open to answers that confuse them. Be careful then, that you do not get the appellation of indolent; and, if possible, avoid the character of frivolous. For,

THE frivolous mind is always busied upon nothing. It mistakes trifling objects for important ones, and spends that time upon little matters, that should only be bestowed upon great ones. Knick-knacks, butterflies, shells, and such like, engross the attention of the frivolous man, and fill up all his time. He studies the dress and not the characters of men, and his subjects of conversation are no other than the weather, his own domestic affairs, his servants, his method of managing his family, the little anecdotes of the neighbourhood, and the fiddle-faddle stories of the day; void of information, void of improvement. These he relates with emphasis, as interesting matters; in short, he is a male gossip, I appeal to your own feelings now, whether such things do not lessen a man, in the opinion of his acquaintance, and instead of attracting esteem, create disgust.

DIGNITY OF MANNERS.

THERE is a certain dignity of manners, without which the very best characters will not be valued.

ROMPING, loud and frequent laughing, punning, joking, mimickry, waggery, and too great and indiscriminate familiarity, will render any one contemptible, in spite of all his knowledge or his merit. These may constitute a merry fellow, but a merry fellow was never yet respectable. Indiscriminate familiarity, will either offend your superiors, or make you pass for their dependant, or toad-eater, and it will put your inferiors on a degree of equality with you, that may be troublesome.

A JOKE, if it carries a sting along with it, is no longer a joke but an affront; and even if it has no sting, unless its witticism is delicate and facetious, instead of giving pleasure, it will disgust; or, if the company *should* laugh, they will probably laugh at the jester rather than the jest.

PUNNING is a mere playing upon words, and far from being a mark of sense: Thus, were we to say, such a dress is *commodious*, one of these wags would answer *odious*; or, that, whatever it has been, it is now be *commodious*. Others will give us an answer different from what we should expect, without either wit, or the least beauty of thought; as, *'Where's my Lord?'*—*'In his clothes, unless he is in bed.'*—*'How does this wine taste?'*—*'A little moist, I think.'*—*'How is this to be eaten?'*—*'With your mouth;'* and so on, all which (you will readily apprehend) are low and vulgar. If your witticisms are not instantly approved by the laugh of the company, for heaven's sake, don't attempt to be witty for the future; for you may take it for granted, the defect is in yourself, and not in your hearers.

AS to a mimick or a wag, he is little else than a buffoon, who will distort his mouth and his eyes to make people laugh. Be assured, no one person ever demeaned himself to please the rest, unless he wished to be thought the Merry-Andrew of the company, and whether this character is respectable, I will leave you to judge.

IF a man's company is coveted on any other account than his knowledge, his good sense, or his manners, he is seldom respected by those who invite him, but made use of only to entertain. 'Let's have such-a-one, for he sings a good song, or he is always joking or laughing;' or 'Let's send for such-a-one, for he is a good bottle companion;' these are degrading distinctions, that preclude all respect and esteem. Whoever is had (as the phrase is) for the sake of any qualification singly, is merely that thing he is had for, is never considered in any other light, and, of course, never properly respected, let his intrinsic merits be what they will.

YOU may possibly suppose this dignity of manners to border upon pride; but it differs as much from pride, as true courage from blustering.

TO flatter a person right or wrong, is abject flattery, and to consent readily to do every thing proposed by a company, be it silly or criminal, is full as degrading, as to dispute warmly upon every subject, and to contradict upon all occasions. To preserve dignity, we should modestly assert our own sentiments, though we politely acquiesce in those of others.

SO again, to support dignity of character, we should neither be frivolously curious about trifles, nor be laboriously intent upon little objects that deserve not a moment's attention; for this implies an incapacity in matters of greater importance.

A GREAT deal likewise depends upon our air, address and expressions; an awkward address and vulgar expressions infer either a low turn of mind, or low education.

INSOLENT contempt, or low envy, is incompatible also with dignity of manners. Low-bred persons, fortunately lifted in the world in fine clothes and fine equipages, will insolently look down on all those who cannot afford to make as good an appearance, and they openly envy those who perhaps make a better. They also dread the being slighted; of course, are suspicious and captious; are uneasy themselves, and make every body else so about them.

A CERTAIN degree of outward seriousness in looks and actions gives dignity, while a constant smirk upon the face (that insipid silly smile, which fools have when they would be civil) and whiffling motions, are strong marks of futility.

BUT above all a dignity of character is to be acquired best by a certain firmness in all our actions. A mean, timid and passive complaisance, lets a man down more than he is aware of; but still his firmness and resolution should not extend to brutality, but be accompanied with a peculiar and engaging softness, or mildness.

IF you discover any hastiness in your temper, and find it apt to break out into rough and unguarded expressions, watch it narrowly, and endeavour to curb it; but let no complaisance, no weak desire of pleasing, no wheedling, urge you to do that which discretion forbids; but persist and persevere in all that is right. In your connexions and friendships, you will find this rule of use to you. Invite and preserve attachments by your firmness; but labour to keep clear of enemies by a mildness of behaviour. Disarm those enemies you may unfortunately have (and few are without them) by a gentleness of manner, but make them feel the steadiness of your just resentment! For there is a wide difference between bearing malice and a determined self-defence; the one is imperious, but the other is prudent and justifiable.

IN directing your servants, or any person you have a right to command; if you deliver your orders mildly, and in that engaging manner which every gentleman should study to do, you would be cheerfully, and consequently, well obeyed; but if tyrannically, you would be very unwillingly served, if served at all. A cool, steady determination should shew that you will be obeyed, but a gentleness in the manner of enforcing that obedience should make your service a cheerful one. Thus will you be loved without being despised, and feared without being hated.

I HOPE I need not mention vices. A man who has patiently been kicked out of company, may have as good a pretence to courage, as one rendered infamous by his vices, may to dignity of any kind; however, of such consequence are appearances, that an outward decency and an affected dignity of manners will even keep such a man the longer from sinking. If therefore you should unfortunately have no intrinsic merit of your own, keep up, if possible, the appearance of it; and the world will possibly give you credit for the rest. A versatility of manners is as necessary in social life, as a versatility of parts in political. This is no way blamable, if not used with an ill design. We must, like the cameleon, often put on the hue of persons we wish to be well with; and it surely can never be blamable, to endeavour to gain the good will or affection of any one, if when obtained, we do not mean to abuse it.

RULES FOR CONVERSATION.

HAVING now given you full and sufficient instructions for making you well received in the best companies; nothing remains but that I lay before you some few rules for your conduct in such company. Many things on this subject I have mentioned before, but some few matters remain to be mentioned now.

1. TALK, then, frequently but not long together, lest you tire the persons you are speaking to; for few persons talk so well upon a subject, as to keep up the attention of their hearers for any length of time.

2. AVOID telling stories in company, unless they are very short indeed, and very applicable to the subject you are upon; in this case relate them in as few words as possible, without the least digression, and with some apology; as that you hate the telling of stories, but the shortness of it induced you. And, if your story has any wit in it, be particularly careful not to laugh at it yourself. Nothing is more tiresome and disagreeable than a long tedious narrative; it betrays a gossiping disposition, and great want of imagination; and nothing is more ridiculous than to express an approbation of your own story, by a laugh.

3. IN relating any thing, keep clear of repetitions, or very hackneyed expressions, such as, *says he*, or *says she*. Some people will use these so often, as to take off the hearer's attention from the story; as, in an organ out of tune, one pipe shall perhaps sound the whole time we are playing, and confuse the piece, so as not to be understood.

4. DIGRESSIONS, likewise, should be guarded against. A story is always more agreeable without them. Of this kind are, *'the gentleman I am telling you of, is the son of Sir Thomas,—who lives in Harley street; you must know him—his brother had a horse that won the sweep stakes at the last Newmarket meeting—Zounds! if you don't know him you know nothing.'* Or, *'He was an upright tall old gentleman, who wore his own long hair: don't you recollect him?'* All this is unnecessary; is very tiresome and provoking, and would be an excuse for a man's behaviour, if he was to leave us in the midst of our narrative.

5. SOME people have a trick of holding the persons they are speaking to by the button, or the hand, in order to be heard out; conscious, I suppose, that their tale is tiresome. Pray, never do this; if the person you speak to is not as willing to hear your story, as you are to tell it, you had much better break off in the middle; for if you tire them once, they will be afraid to listen to you a second time.

6. OTHERS have a way of punching the person they are talking to, in the side, and at the end of every sentence, asking him some such questions as the following: 'Wasn't I right in that?'—'You know, I told you so?'—'What's your opinion?' and the like; or perhaps they will be thrusting him, or jogging him with their elbow. For mercy's sake, never give way to this; it will make your company dreaded.

7. LONG talkers are frequently apt to single out some unfortunate man present, generally the most silent one of the company, or probably him who sits next to him. To this man, in a kind of half-whisper they will run on for half an hour together. Nothing can be more ill-bred. But if one of these unmerciful talkers should attack you, if you wish to oblige him, I would recommend the hearing him with patience: Seem to do so at least, for you could not hurt him more than to leave him in the middle of his story, or discover any impatience in the course of it.

8. INCESSANT talkers are very disagreeable companions. Nothing can be more rude than to engross the conversation to yourself, or to take the words as it were, out of another man's mouth. Every man in company has an equal claim to bear his part in the conversation, and to deprive him of it, is not only unjust, but a tacit declaration that he cannot speak so well upon the subject as yourself; you will therefore take it up: And, what can be more rude? I would as soon forgive a man that should stop my mouth when I was gaping, as take my words from me while I was speaking them. Now, if this be unpardonable, it cannot be less so

9. TO help out or forestal the slow speaker, as if you alone were rich in expressions, and he were poor. You may take it for granted, every one is vain enough to think he can talk well, though he may modestly deny it; helping a person therefore out in his expressions, is a correction that will stamp the corrector with impudence and ill manners.

10. THOSE who contradict others upon all occasions, and make every assertion a matter of dispute, betray by this behaviour an unacquaintance with good-breeding. He therefore who wishes to appear amiable, with those he converses with, will be cautious of such expressions as these, 'That can't be true, Sir.' 'The affair is as I say.' 'That must be false, Sir.' 'If what you say is true, &c.' You may as well tell a man he lies at once, as thus indirectly impeach his veracity. It is equally as rude to be proving every trifling assertion with a bet or a wager. 'I'll bet you fifty of it, and so on.' Make it then a constant rule, in matters of no great importance, complaisantly to submit your opinion to that of others; for a victory of this kind often costs a man the loss of a friend.

11. GIVING advice unasked, is another piece of rudeness; it is, in effect, declaring ourselves wiser than those to whom we give it; reproaching them

with ignorance and inexperience. It is a freedom that ought not to be taken with any common acquaintance, and yet there are those, who will be offended, if their advice is not taken. 'Such-a-one,' say they, 'is above being advised.' 'He scorns to listen to my advice;' as if it were not a mark of greater arrogance to expect every one to submit to their opinion, than for a man sometimes to follow his own.

12. THERE is nothing so unpardonably rude as a seeming inattention to the person who is speaking to you; though you may meet with it in others, by all means, avoid it yourself. Some ill-bred people, while others are speaking to them, will, instead of looking at, or attending to them, perhaps fix their eyes on the ceiling, or some picture in the room, look out of a window, play with a dog, their watch chain, or their cane, or probably pick their nails or their noses. Nothing betrays a more trifling mind than this; nor can any thing be a greater affront to the person speaking; it being a tacit declaration, that what he is saying is not worth your attention. Consider with yourself how you would like such treatment, and, I am persuaded you will never shew it to others.

13. SURLINESS or moroseness is incompatible also with politeness. Such as, should any one say 'he was desired to present Mr. Such-a-one's respects to you,' to reply, 'What the devil have I to do with his respects?' 'My Lord enquired after you lately, and asked how you did,' to answer, 'If he wishes to know, let him come and feel my pulse;' and the like. A good deal of this often is affected; but whether affected or natural, it is always offensive. A man of this stamp will occasionally be laughed at, as an oddity; but in the end will be despised.

14. I SHOULD suppose it unnecessary to advise you to adapt your conversation to the company you are in. You would not surely start the same subject, and discourse of it in the same manner with the old and with the young, with an officer, a clergyman, a philosopher, and a woman. No; your good sense will undoubtedly teach you to be serious with the serious, gay with the gay, and to trifle with the triflers.

15. THERE are certain expressions which are exceedingly rude, and yet there are people of liberal education that sometimes use them; as 'You don't understand me, Sir,' 'It is not so.' 'You mistake.' 'You know nothing of the matter, &c.' Is it not better to say? 'I believe, I do not express myself so as to be understood.' 'Let us consider it again, whether we take it right or not.' It is much more polite and amiable to make some excuse for another, even in cases where he might justly be blamed, and to represent the mistake as common to both, rather than charge him with insensibility or incomprehension.

16. IF anyone should have promised you any thing, and not have fulfilled that promise, it would be very unpolite to tell him, he has forfeited his word; or if the same person should have disappointed you, upon any occasion, would it not be better to say, 'You were probably so much engaged, that you forgot my affair;' or, 'Perhaps it slipped your memory;' rather than, 'You thought no more about it,' or 'you pay very little regard to your word.' For, expressions of this kind leave a sting behind them. They are a kind of provocation and affront, and very often bring on lasting quarrels.

17. BE careful not to appear dark and mysterious, lest you should be thought suspicious; than which there cannot be a more unamiable character. If you appear mysterious and reserved, others will be truly so with you; and in this case there is an end to improvement, for you will gather no information. Be reserved, but never seem so.

18. THERE is a fault extremely common with some people, which I would have *you* to avoid. When their opinion is asked, upon any subject, they will give it with so apparent a diffidence and timidity, that one cannot, without the utmost pain, listen to them; especially if they are known to be men of universal knowledge. 'Your Lordship will pardon me,' says one of this stamp, 'if I should not be able to speak to the case in hand, so well as it might be wished.'—'I'll venture to speak of this matter to the best of my poor abilities and dulness of apprehension.'—'I fear I shall expose myself, but in obedience to your Lordship's commands'—and while they are making these apologies, they interrupt the business and tire the company.

19. ALWAYS look people in the face, when you speak to them, otherwise you will be thought conscious of some guilt, besides, you lose the opportunity of reading their countenances, from which you will much better learn the impression your discourse makes upon them than you can possibly do from their words; for words are at the will of every one, but the countenance is frequently involuntary.

20. IF in speaking to a person, you are not heard, and should be desired to repeat what you said, do not raise your voice in the repetition, lest you should be thought angry, on being obliged to repeat what you said before; it was probably owing to the hearer's inattention.

21. ONE word only, as to swearing. Those who addict themselves to it, and interlard their discourse with oaths, can never be considered as gentlemen; they are generally people of low education, and are unwelcome in what is called good company. It is a vice that has no temptation to plead, but is, in every respect, as vulgar as it is wicked.

22. NEVER accustom yourself to scandal, nor listen to it; for though it may gratify the malevolence of some people, nine times out of ten, it is attended with great disadvantages. The very persons you tell it to, will, on reflection, entertain a mean opinion of you, and it will often bring you into very disagreeable situations. And as there would be no evil speakers, if there were no evil hearers, it is in scandal as in robbery; the receiver is as bad as the thief. Besides, it will lead people to shun your company, supposing that you will speak ill of them to the next acquaintance you meet.

23. MIMICKRY, the favourite amusement of little minds, has been ever the contempt of great ones. Never give way to it yourself, nor ever encourage it in others; it is the most illiberal of all buffoonery; it is an insult on the person you mimick; and insults, I have often told you, are seldom forgiven.

24. CAREFULLY avoid talking either of your own or other people's domestic concerns. By doing the one, you will be thought vain; by entering into the other, you will be considered as officious. Talking of yourself is an impertinence to the company; your affairs are nothing to them; besides they cannot be kept too secret. And as to the affairs of others, what are they to you? In talking of matters that no way concern you, you are liable to commit blunders, and should you touch any one in a sore part, you may possibly lose his esteem. Let your conversation, then, in mixed companies, always be general.

25. JOKES, bon-mots, or the little pleasantries of one company, will not often bear to be told in another; they are frequently local, and take their rise from certain circumstances, a second company may not be acquainted with; these circumstances, and of course your story, may be misunderstood, or want explaining; and if after you have prefaced it with,—'I will tell you a good thing;'—the sting should not be immediately perceived, you will appear exceedingly ridiculous, and wish you had not told it. Never then without caution repeat in one place, what you hear in another.

26. IN most debates, take up the favourable side of the question; however, let me caution you against being clamorous, that is, never maintain an argument with heat, though you know yourself right; but offer your sentiments modestly and coolly, and if this does not prevail, give it up, and try to change the subject by saying something to this effect—'I find we shall hardly convince one another, neither is there any necessity to attempt it; so let us talk of something else.'

27. NOT that I would have you give up your opinion always; no, assert your own sentiments, and oppose those of others, when wrong; but let your manner and voice be gentle and engaging, and yet no ways affected. If you contradict, do it with, 'I may be wrong, I won't be positive, but I really think—I should rather suppose—If I may be permitted to say,' and close

your dispute with good humour, to shew that you are neither displeased yourself nor meant to displease the person you dispute with.

28. ACQUAINT yourself with the character and situations of the company you go into, before you give a loose to your tongue; for, should you enlarge on some virtue, which any one present may notoriously want; or should you condemn some vice, which any of the company may be particularly addicted to, they will be apt to think your reflections pointed and personal, and you will be sure to give offence. This consideration will naturally lead you, not to suppose things said in general, to be leveled at you.

29. LOW-BRED people, when they happen occasionally to be in good company, imagine themselves to be the subject of every separate conversation. If any part of the company whisper, it is about them; if they laugh, it is at them; and if any thing is said which they do not comprehend, they immediately suppose it is meant of them. This mistake is admirably ridiculed in one of our celebrated comedies, 'I am sure,' says Scrub, 'they were talking of me, for they laughed consumedly.' Now, a well-bred person never thinks himself disesteemed by the company, or laughed at, unless their reflections are so gross, that he cannot be supposed to mistake them, and his honour obliges him to resent it in a proper manner; however, be assured, gentlemen never laugh at, or ridicule one another, unless they are in joke, or on a footing of the greatest intimacy. If such a thing should happen once in an age, from some pert coxcomb, or some flippant woman, it is better to seem not to know it, than to make the least reply.

30. IT is a piece of politeness not to interrupt a person in a story, whether you have heard it before or not. Nay, if a well-bred man is asked whether he has heard it; he will answer no, and let the person go on, though he knows it already. Some are fond of telling a story, because they think they tell it well, others pride themselves in being the first teller of it, and others are pleased at being thought entrusted with it. Now, all these persons you would disappoint by answering yes. And, as I have told you before, as the greatest proof of politeness is to make every body happy about you, I would never deprive a person of any secret satisfaction of this sort, in which I could gratify him by a minute's attention.

31. BE not ashamed of asking questions, if such questions lead to information; always accompany them with some excuse, and you never will be reckoned impertinent. But abrupt questions, without some apology, by all means avoid, as they imply design. There is a way of fishing for facts, which, if done judiciously, will answer every purpose, such as, taking things you wish to know for granted; this will perhaps lead some officious person to set you right. So again, by saying, you have heard so and so, and sometimes seeming to know more than you do, you will often get at

information, which you would lose by direct questions, as these would put people on their guard, and frequently defeat the very end you aim at.

32. MAKE it a rule never to reflect on any body of people, for, reflections of this nature create many enemies. There are good and bad of all professions; lawyers, soldiers, parsons, or citizens. They are all men, subject to the same passions, differing only in their manner, according to the way they have been bred up in. For this reason, it is unjust, as well as indiscreet, to attack them as a CORPS collectively. Many a young man has thought himself extremely clever in abusing the clergy. What are the clergy more than other men? Can you suppose a black gown can make any alteration in his nature? Fie, fie; think seriously, and I am convinced you will never do it.

33. BUT above all, let no example, no fashion, no witticism, no foolish desire of rising above what knaves call prejudices, tempt you to excuse, extenuate or ridicule the least breach of morality; but upon every occasion, shew the greatest abhorrence of such proceedings, and hold virtue and religion in the highest veneration.

34. IT is a great piece of ill-manners to interrupt any one while speaking, by speaking yourself, or calling off the attention of the company to any foreign matter. But this every child knows.

35. THE last thing I shall mention is that of concealing your learning, except on particular occasions. Reserve this for learned men, and let them rather extort it from you, than you be too willing to display it. Hence you will be thought modest, and to have more knowledge than you really have. Never seem wise or more learned than the company you are in. He who affects to shew his learning, will be frequently questioned; and if found superficial, will be sneered at; if otherwise, he will be deemed a pedant. Real merit will always shew itself, and nothing can lessen it in the opinion of the world, but a man's exhibiting it himself.

FOR God's sake, revolve all these things seriously in your mind, before you go abroad into life. Recollect the observations you have yourself occasionally made upon men and things, compare them with my instructions, and act wisely, and consequently, as they shall teach you.

A FATHER'S LEGACY TO HIS DAUGHTERS.

MY DEAR GIRLS,

YOU had the misfortune to be deprived of your mother, at a time of life when you were insensible of your loss, and could receive little benefit, either from her instruction, or her example. Before this comes to your hands, you will likewise have lost your father.

I HAVE had many melancholy reflections on the forlorn and helpless situation you must be in, if it should please God to remove me from you before you arrive at that period of life, when you will be able to think and act for yourselves. I know mankind too well. I know their falsehood, their dissipation, their coldness to all the duties of friendship and humanity. I know the little attention paid to helpless infancy. You will meet with few friends disinterested enough to do you good offices, when you are incapable of making them any return, by contributing to their interest or their pleasure, or to the gratification of their vanity.

I HAVE been supported under the gloom naturally arising from these reflections, by a reliance on the goodness of that Providence which has hitherto preferred you, and given me the most pleasing prospect of the goodness of your dispositions; and by the secret hope, that your mother's virtues will entail a blessing on her children.

THE anxiety I have for your happiness has made me resolve to throw together my sentiments, relating to your future conduct in life. If I live for some years, you will receive them with much greater advantage, suited to your different geniuses and dispositions. If I die sooner, you must receive them in this very imperfect manner,—the last proof of my affection.

YOU will all remember your father's fondness, when perhaps every other circumstance relating to him is forgotten. This remembrance, I hope, will induce you to give a serious attention to the advices I am now going to leave with you.—I can request this attention with the greater confidence, as my sentiments on the most interesting points that regard life and manners, were entirely correspondent to your mother's, whose judgment and taste I trusted much more than my own.

YOU must expect that the advice which I shall give you will be very imperfect, as there are many nameless delicacies, in female manners, of which none but a woman can judge.

YOU will have one advantage by attending to what I am going to leave with you; you will hear, at least for once in your lives, the genuine sentiments of a man, who has no interest in flattering or deceiving you.—I shall throw my reflections together without any studied order, and shall only, to avoid confusion range them under a few general heads.

YOU will see, in a little treatise of mine just published, in what an honourable point of view I have considered your sex; not as domestic drudges, or the slaves of our pleasures, but as our companions and equals; as designed to soften our hearts and polish our manners; and as Thomson finely says,

To raise the virtues, animate the bliss,

And sweeten all the toils of human life.

I shall not repeat what I have there said on this subject, and shall only observe, that from the view I have given of your natural character and place in society, there arises a certain propriety of conduct peculiar to your sex. It is this peculiar propriety of female manners of which I intend to give you my sentiments, without touching on those general rules of conduct by which men and women are equally bound.

WHILE I explain to you that system of conduct which I think will tend most to your honour and happiness, I shall, at the same time, endeavour to point out those virtues and accomplishment which render you most respectable and most amiable in the eyes of my own sex.

RELIGION.

THOUGH the duties of religion, strictly speaking, are equally binding on both sexes, yet certain differences in their natural character and education, render some vices in your sex particularly odious. The natural hardiness of our hearts, and strength of our passions, inflamed by the uncontrouled license we are too often indulged with in our youth, are apt to render our manners more dissolute, and make us less susceptible of the finer feelings of the heart. Your superior delicacy, your modesty, and the usual severity of your education, preserve you, in a great measure, from any temptation to those vices to which we are most subjected. The natural softness and sensibility of your dispositions particularly fit you for the practice of those duties where the heart is chiefly concerned. And this, along with the natural warmth of your imaginations, renders you peculiarly susceptible of the feelings of devotion.

THERE are many circumstances in your situation that peculiarly require the supports of religion to enable you to act in them with spirit and propriety. Your whole life is often a life of suffering. You cannot plunge into business, or dissipate yourselves in pleasure and riot, as men too often do, when under the pressure of misfortunes. You must bear your sorrows in silence, unknown and unpitied. You must often put on a face of serenity and cheerfulness, when your hearts are torn with anguish, or sinking in despair. Then your only resource is in the consolations of religion. It is chiefly owing to these that you bear domestic misfortunes better than we do.

BUT you are sometimes in very different circumstances, that equally require the restraints of religion. The natural vivacity, and perhaps the natural vanity of your sex, are very apt to lead you into a dissipated state of life, that deceives you, under the appearance of innocent pleasure; but which in reality wastes your spirits, impairs your health, weakens all the superior faculties of your minds, and often sullies your reputations. Religion by checking this dissipation and rage for pleasure, enables you to draw more happiness, even from those very sources of amusement, which when too frequently applied to, are often productive of satiety and disgust.

RELIGION is rather a matter of sentiment than reasoning. The important and interesting articles of faith are sufficiently plain. Fix your attention on these, and do not meddle with controversy. If you get into that, you plunge into a chaos, from which you will never be able to extricate yourselves. It spoils the temper, and, I suspect, has no good effect on the heart.

AVOID all books, and all conversation, that tend to shake your faith on those great points of religion which should serve to regulate your conduct, and on which your hopes of future and eternal happiness depend.

NEVER indulge yourselves in ridicule on religious subjects; nor give countenance to it in others, by seeming diverted with what they say. This, to people of good-breeding, will be a sufficient check.

I WISH you to go no farther than the Scriptures for your religious opinions. Embrace those you find clearly revealed. Never perplex yourselves about such as you do not understand, but treat them with silent and becoming reverence.—I would advise you to read only such religious books as are addressed to the heart; such as inspire pious and devout affections, such as are proper to direct you in your conduct, and not such as tend to entangle you in the endless maze of opinions and systems.

BE punctual in the stated performance of your private devotions morning and evening. If you have any sensibility or imagination, this will establish such an intercourse between you and the Supreme Being, as will be of infinite consequence to you in life. It will communicate an habitual cheerfulness to your tempers; give a firmness and steadiness to your virtue, and enable you to go through all the vicissitudes of human life with propriety and dignity.

I WISH you to be regular in your attendance on public worship, and in receiving the communion. Allow nothing to interrupt your public or private devotions, except the performance of some active duty in life, to which they should always give place.—In your behaviour at public worship, observe an exemplary attention and gravity.

THAT extreme strictness which I recommend to you in these duties, will be considered by many of your acquaintance as a superstitious attachment to forms; but in the advice I give you on this and other subjects, I have an eye to the spirit and manners of the age. There is a levity and dissipation in the present manners, a coldness and listlessness in whatever relates to religion, which cannot fail to infect you, unless you purposely cultivate in your minds a contrary bias, and make the devotional taste habitual.

AVOID all grimace and ostentation in your religious duties. They are the usual cloaks of hypocrisy; at least they shew a weak and vain mind.

DO not make religion a subject of common conversation in mixed companies. When it is introduced, rather seem to decline it. At the same time, never suffer any person to insult you by any foolish ribaldry on your religious opinions, but shew the same resentment you would naturally do on being offered any other personal insult. But the surest way to avoid this, is by a modest reserve on the subject, and by using no freedom with others about their religious sentiments.

CULTIVATE an enlarged charity for all mankind, however they may differ from you in their religious opinions. That difference may probably arise from causes in which you had no share, and from which you can derive no merit.

SHEW your regard to religion, by a distinguishing respect to all its ministers, of whatever persuasion, who do not by their lives dishonour their profession; but never allow them the direction of your consciences lest they taint you with the narrow spirit of their party.

THE best effect of your religion will be a diffusive humanity to all in distress.—Set apart a certain proportion of your income as sacred to charitable purposes. But in this, as well as in the practice of every other duty, carefully avoid ostentation. Vanity is always defeating her own purposes. Fame is one of the natural rewards of virtue. Do not pursue her, and she will follow you.

DO not confine your charity to giving money. You may have many opportunities of shewing a tender and compassionate spirit where your money is not wanted.—There is a false and unnatural refinement in sensibility, which makes some people shun the sight of every object in distress. Never indulge this, especially where your friends or acquaintances are concerned. Let the days of their misfortunes, when the world forgets or avoids them, be the season for you to exercise your humanity and friendship. The sight of human misery softens the heart, and makes it better; it checks the pride of health and prosperity, and the distress it occasions is amply compensated by the consciousness of doing your duty, and by the secret endearments which nature has annexed to all our sympathetic sorrows.

WOMEN are greatly deceived, when they think they recommend themselves to our sex by their indifference about religion. Even those men who are themselves unbelievers dislike infidelity in you. Every man who knows human nature, connects a religious taste in your sex with softness and sensibility of heart; at least we always consider the want of it as a proof of that hard and masculine spirit, which of all your faults we dislike the most. Besides, men consider your religion as one of their principal securities for that female virtue in which they are most interested. If a gentleman pretends an attachment to any of you, and endeavours to shake your religious principles, be assured he is either a fool, or has designs on you which he dares not openly avow.

YOU will probably wonder at my having educated you in a church different from my own. The reason was plainly this: I looked on the differences between our churches to be of no real importance, and that a preference of one to the other was a mere matter of taste. Your mother was educated in the church of England, and had an attachment to it, and I had a prejudice in favour of every thing she liked. It never was her desire that you should be baptized by a clergyman of the church of England, or be educated in that church. On the contrary, the delicacy of her regard to the smallest circumstance that could affect me in the eye of the world, made her anxiously insist it might be otherwise. But I could not yield to her in that kind of generality.—When I lost her, I became still more determined to educate you in that church, as I feel a secret pleasure in doing every thing that appears to me to express my affection and veneration for her memory.—I draw but a very faint and imperfect picture of what your mother was, while I endeavour to point out what you should be.[2]

2. The reader will remember, that such observations as respect equally both the sexes are all along as much as possible avoided.

CONDUCT AND BEHAVIOUR.

ONE of the chiefest beauties in a female character is that modest reserve, that retiring delicacy, which avoids the public eye, and is disconcerted even at the gaze of admiration.—I do not wish you to be insensible to applause. If you were, you must become, if not worse, at least less amiable women. But you may be dazzled by that admiration, which yet rejoices your hearts.

WHEN a girl ceases to blush, she has lost the most powerful charm of beauty. That extreme sensibility which it indicates, may be a weakness and incumbrance in our sex, as I have too often felt; but in yours it is peculiarly engaging. Pedants, who think themselves philosophers, ask why a woman should blush when she is conscious of no crime. It is a sufficient answer, that Nature has made you to blush when you are guilty of no fault, and has forced us to love you because you do so.—Blushing is so far from being necessarily an attendant on guilt, that it is the usual companion of innocence.

THIS modesty, which I think so essential in your sex, will naturally dispose you to be rather silent in company, especially in a large one.—People of sense and discernment will never mistake such silence for dulness. One may take a share in conversation without uttering a syllable. The expression in the countenance shews it, and this never escapes an observing eye.

I SHOULD be glad that you had an easy dignity in your behaviour at public places, but not that confident ease, that unabashed countenance, which seems to set the company at defiance.—If, while a gentleman is speaking to you, one of superior rank addresses you, do not let your eager attention and visible preference betray the flutter of your heart. Let your pride on this occasion preserve you from that meanness into which your vanity would sink you. Consider that you expose yourselves to the ridicule of the company, and affront one gentleman only to swell the triumph of another, who perhaps thinks he does you honour in speaking to you.

CONVERSE with men even of the first rank with that dignified modesty, which may prevent the approach of the most distant familiarity, and consequently prevent them from feeling themselves your superiors.

WIT is the most dangerous talent you can possess. It must be guarded with great discretion and good-nature, otherwise it will create you many enemies. It is perfectly consistent with softness and delicacy; yet they are seldom found united. Wit is so flattering to vanity, that those who possess it become intoxicated, and lose all self-command.

HUMOUR is a different quality. It will make your company much solicited; but be cautious how you indulge it.—It is often a great enemy to delicacy, and a still greater one to dignity of character. It may sometimes gain you applause, but will never procure you respect.

BE even cautious in displaying your good sense. It will be thought you assume a superiority over the rest of the company. But if you happen to have any learning, keep it a profound secret, especially from the men, who generally look with a jealous and malignant eye on a woman of great parts, and a cultivated understanding.

A MAN of real genius and candour is far superior to this meanness. But such a one will seldom fall in your way; and if by accident he should, do not be anxious to shew the full extent of your knowledge. If he has any opportunities of seeing you, he will soon discover it himself; and if you have any advantages of person or manner, and keep your own secret, he will probably give you credit for a great deal more than you possess.—The great art of pleasing in conversation consists in making the company pleased with themselves. You will more readily hear than talk yourselves into their good graces.

BEWARE of detraction, especially where your own sex are concerned. You are generally accused of being particularly addicted to this vice; I think unjustly.—Men are fully as guilty of it when their interests interfere. As your interests more frequently clash, and as your feelings are quicker than ours, your temptations to it are more frequent. For this reason, be particularly tender of the reputation of your own sex, especially when they happen to rival you in our regards. We look on this as the strongest proof of dignity and true greatness of mind.

SHEW a compassionate sympathy to unfortunate women, especially to those who are rendered so by the villany of men. Indulge a secret pleasure, I may say pride, in being the friends and refuge of the unhappy, but without the vanity of shewing it.

CONSIDER every species of indelicacy in conversation, as shameful in itself, and as highly disgusting to us. All double entendre is of this sort.—The dissoluteness of men's education allows them to be diverted with a kind of wit, which yet they have delicacy enough to be shocked at, when it comes from your mouths, or even when you hear it without pain and contempt. Virgin purity is of that delicate nature, that it cannot hear certain things without contamination. It is always in your power to avoid these. No man, but a brute or a fool, will insult a woman with conversation which he sees gives her pain; nor will he dare to do it, if she resent the injury with a becoming spirit.—There is a dignity in conscious virtue which is able to awe the most shameless and abandoned of men.

YOU will be reproached perhaps with prudery. By prudery is usually meant an affectation of delicacy. Now I do not wish you to affect delicacy; I wish you to possess it. At any rate, it is better to run the risk of being thought ridiculous than disgusting.

THE men will complain of your reserve. They will assure you, that a franker behaviour would make you more amiable. But trust me, they are not sincere when they tell you so.—I acknowledge, that on some occasions it might render you more agreeable as companions, but it would make you less amiable as women; an important distinction which many of your sex are not aware of.—After all, I wish you to have great ease and openness in your conversation. I only point out some considerations which ought to regulate your behaviour in that respect.

HAVE a sacred regard to truth. Lying is a mean and despicable vice.—I have known some women of excellent parts, who were so much addicted to it, that they could not be trusted in the relation of any story, especially if it contained any thing of the marvellous, or if they themselves were the heroines of the tale. This weakness did not proceed from a bad heart, but was merely the effect of vanity, or an unbridled imagination.—I do not mean to censure that lively embellishment of a humorous story, which is only intended to promote innocent mirth.

THERE is a certain gentleness of spirit and manners extremely engaging in your sex; not that indiscriminate attention, that unmeaning simper, which smiles on all alike. This arises, either from an affectation of softness, or from perfect insipidity.

THERE is a species of refinement in luxury, just beginning to prevail among the gentlemen of this country, to which our ladies are yet as great strangers as any women upon earth; I hope, for the honour of the sex, they may ever continue so: I mean, the luxury of eating. It is a despicable selfish vice in men, but in your sex it is beyond expression indelicate and disgusting.

EVERY one who remembers a few years back, is sensible of a very striking change in the attention and respect formerly paid by the gentlemen to the ladies. Their drawing-rooms are deserted; and after dinner and supper, the gentlemen are impatient till they retire. How they came to lose this respect, which nature and politeness so well intitle them to, I shall not here particularly inquire. The revolutions of manners in any country depend on causes very various and complicated. I shall only observe, that the behaviour of the ladies in the last age was very reserved and stately. It would now be reckoned ridiculously stiff and formal. Whatever it was, it had certainly the effect of making them more respected.

A FINE woman, like other fine things in nature, has her proper point of view, from which she may be seen to most advantage. To fix this point requires great judgment, and an intimate knowledge of the human heart. By the present mode of female manners, the ladies seem to expect that they shall regain their ascendancy over us, by the fullest display of their personal charms, by being always in our eye at public places, by conversing with us with the same unreserved freedom as we do with one another; in short, by resembling us as nearly as they possibly can.—But a little time and experience will shew the folly of this expectation and conduct.

THE power of a fine woman over the hearts of men, men of the finest parts, is even beyond what she conceives. They are sensible of the pleasing illusion, but they cannot, nor do they wish to dissolve it. But if she is determined to dispel the charm, it certainly is in her power: she may soon reduce the angel to a very ordinary girl.

THERE is a native dignity, an ingenuous modesty to be expected in your sex, which is your natural protection from the familiarities of the men, and which you should feel previous to the reflection that it is your interest to keep yourselves sacred from all personal freedoms. The many nameless charms and endearments of beauty should be reserved to bless the arms of the happy man to whom you give your heart, but who, if he has the least delicacy, will despise them, if he knows that they have been prostituted to fifty men before him.—The sentiment, that a woman may allow all innocent freedoms, provided her virtue is secure, is both grossly indelicate and dangerous, and has proved fatal to many of your sex.

LET me now recommend to your attention that elegance, which is not so much a quality itself, as the high polish of every other. It is what diffuses an ineffable grace over every look, every motion, every sentence you utter. It gives that charm to beauty without which it generally fails to please. It is partly a personal quality, in which respect it is the gift of nature; but I speak of it principally as a quality of the mind. In a word, it is the perfection of taste in life and manners;—every virtue and every excellence, in their most graceful and amiable forms.

YOU may perhaps think that I want to throw every spark of nature out of your composition, and to make you entirely artificial. Far from it. I wish you to possess the most perfect simplicity of heart and manners. I think you may possess dignity without pride, affability without meanness, and simple elegance without affectation. Milton had my idea, when he says of Eve,

Grace was in all her steps, Heaven in her eye, In every gesture dignity and love.

AMUSEMENTS.

EVERY period of life has amusements which are natural and proper to it. You may indulge the variety of your tastes in these, while you keep within the bounds of that propriety which is suitable to your sex.

SOME amusements are conducive to health, as various kinds of exercise: some are connected with qualities really useful, as different kinds of women's work, and all the domestic concerns of a family: some are elegant accomplishments, as dress, dancing, music, and drawing. Such books as improve your understanding, enlarge your knowledge, and cultivate your taste, may be considered in a higher point of view than mere amusements. There are a variety of others, which are neither useful nor ornamental, such as play of different kinds.

I WOULD particularly recommend to you those exercises that oblige you to be much abroad in the open air, such as walking, and riding on horse back. This will give vigour to your constitutions, and a bloom to your complexions. If you accustom yourselves to go abroad always in chairs and carriages, you will soon become so enervated, as to be unable to go out of doors without them. They are like most articles of luxury, useful and agreeable when judiciously used; but when made habitual, they become both insipid and pernicious.

AN attention to your health is a duty you owe to yourselves and to your friends. Bad health seldom fails to have an influence on the spirits and temper. The finest geniuses, the most delicate minds, have very frequently a correspondent delicacy of bodily constitutions, which they are too apt to neglect. Their luxury lies in reading and late hours, equal enemies to health and beauty.

BUT though good health be one of the greatest blessings of life, never make a boast of it, but enjoy it in grateful silence. We so naturally associate the idea of female softness and delicacy with a correspondent delicacy of constitution, that when a woman speaks of her great strength, her extraordinary appetite, her ability to bear excessive fatigue, we recoil at the description in a way she is little aware of.

THE intention of your being taught needlework, knitting, and such like, is not on account of the intrinsic value of all you can do with your hands, which is trifling, but to enable you to judge more perfectly of that kind of work, and to direct the execution of it in others. Another principal end is to enable you to fill up, in a tolerably agreeable way, some of the many solitary hours you must necessarily pass at home. It is a great article in the happiness of life, to have your pleasures as independent of others as possible. By continually gadding abroad in search of amusement, you lose the respect of all your acquaintances, whom you oppress with those visits, which, by a more discreet management, might have been courted.

THE domestic economy of a family is entirely a woman's province, and furnishes a variety of subjects for the exertion both of good sense and good taste. If you ever come to have the charge of a family, it ought to engage much of your time and attention; nor can you be excused from this by any extent of fortune, though with a narrow one the ruin that follows the neglect of it may be more immediate.

I AM at the greatest loss what to advise you in regard to books. There is no impropriety in your reading history, or cultivating any art or science to which genius or accident leads you. The whole volume of Nature lies open to your eye, and furnishes an infinite variety of entertainment. If I was sure that nature had given you such strong principles of taste and sentiment as would remain with you, and influence your future conduct, with the utmost pleasure would I endeavour to direct your reading in such a way as might form that taste to the utmost perfection of truth and elegance. "But when I reflect how easy it is to warm a girl's imagination, and how difficult deeply and permanently to affect her heart; how readily she enters into every refinement of sentiment, and how easily she can sacrifice them to vanity or convenience;" I think I may very probably do you an injury by artificially creating a taste, which, if Nature never gave it you, would only serve to embarrass your future conduct.—I do not want to *make* you any thing: I want to know what Nature has made you, and to perfect you on her plan. I do not wish you to have sentiments that might perplex you: I wish you to have sentiments that may uniformly and steadily guide you, and such as your hearts so thoroughly approve, that you would not forego them for any consideration this world could offer.

DRESS is an important article in female life. The love of dress is natural to you, and therefore it is proper and reasonable. Good sense will regulate your expence in it, and good taste will direct you to dress in such a way as to conceal any blemishes, and set off your beauties, if you have any, to the greatest advantage. But much delicacy and judgement are required in the application of this rule. A fine woman shews her charms to most advantage, when she seems most to conceal them. The finest bosom in nature is not so fine as what imagination forms. The most perfect elegance of dress appears always the most easy, and the least studied.

DO not confine your attention to dress to your public appearances. Accustom yourselves to an habitual neatness, so that in the most careless undress, in your unguarded hours, you may have no reason to be ashamed of your appearance.—You will not easily believe how much we consider your dress as expressive of your characters. Vanity, levity, slovenliness, folly, appear through it. An elegant simplicity is an equal proof of taste and delicacy.

IN dancing, the principal points you are to attend to are ease and grace. I would have you to dance with spirit; but never allow yourselves to be so far transported with mirth, as to forget the delicacy of your sex.—Many a girl dancing in the gaiety and innocence of her heart, is thought to discover a spirit she little dreams of.

I KNOW no entertainment that gives such pleasure to any person of sentiment or humour, as the theatre. But I am sorry to say, there are few English comedies a lady can see, without a shock to delicacy. You will not readily suspect the comments gentlemen make on your behaviour on such occasions. Men are often best acquainted with the most worthless of your sex, and from them too readily form their judgment of the rest. A virtuous girl often hears very indelicate things with a countenance no wise embarrassed, because in truth she does not understand them. Yet this is, most ungenerously, ascribed to that command of features, and that ready presence of mind, which you are thought to possess in a degree far beyond us; or, by still more malignant observers, it is ascribed to hardened effrontery.

SOMETIMES a girl laughs with all the simplicity of unsuspecting innocence, for no other reason but being infected with other people's laughing: she is then believed to know more than she should do.—If she does happen to understand an improper thing, she suffers a very complicated distress: she feels her modesty hurt in the most sensible manner, and at the same time is ashamed of appearing conscious of the injury. The only way to avoid these inconveniencies, is never to go to a play that is particularly offensive to delicacy.—Tragedy subjects you to no such distress.—Its sorrows will soften and ennoble your hearts.

I NEED say little about gaming, the ladies in this country being as yet almost strangers to it. It is a ruinous and incurable vice; and as it leads to all the selfish and turbulent passions, is peculiarly odious in your sex. I have no objection to your playing a little at any kind of game, as a variety in your amusements, provided that what you can possibly lose is such a trifle as can neither interest nor hurt you.

IN this, as well as in all important points of conduct, shew a determined resolution and steadiness. This is not in the least inconsistent with that softness and gentleness so amiable in your sex. On the contrary, it gives that spirit to a mild and sweet disposition, without which it is apt to degenerate into insipidity. It makes you respectable in your own eyes, and dignifies you in ours.

FRIENDSHIP, LOVE, MARRIAGE.

THE luxury and dissipation that prevail in genteel life, as they corrupt the heart in many respects, so they render it incapable of warm, sincere, and steady friendship. A happy choice of friends will be of the utmost consequence to you, as they may assist you by their advice and good offices. But the immediate gratification which friendship affords to a warm, open and ingenuous heart, is of itself a sufficient motive to court it.

IN the choice of your friends, have principal regard to goodness of heart and fidelity. If they also possess taste and genius, that will still make them more agreeable and useful companions. You have particular reason to place confidence in those who have shewn affection for you in your early days, when you were incapable of making them any return. This is an obligation for which you cannot be too grateful: When you read this, you will naturally think of your mother's friend, to whom you owe so much.

IF you have the good fortune to meet with any who deserve the name of friends, unbosom yourself to them with the most unsuspicious confidence. It is one of the world's maxims, never to trust any person with a secret, the discovery of which could give you any pain; but it is the maxim of a little mind and a cold heart, unless where it is the effect of frequent disappointments and bad usage. An open temper, if restrained but by tolerable prudence, will make you, on the whole, much happier than a reserved suspicious one, although you may sometimes suffer by it. Coldness and distrust are but the too certain consequences of age and experience; but they are unpleasant feelings, and need not be anticipated before their time.

BUT however open you may be in talking of your own affairs, never disclose the secrets of one friend to another. These are sacred deposites, which do not belong to you, nor have you any right to make use of them.

THERE is another case, in which I suspect it is proper to be secret, not so much from motives of prudence, as delicacy. I mean in love matters. Though a woman has no reason to be ashamed of an attachment to a man of merit, yet nature, whose authority is superior to philosophy, has annexed a sense of shame to it. It is even long before a woman of delicacy dares avow to her own heart that she loves; and when all the subterfuges of ingenuity to conceal it from herself fail, she feels a violence done both to her pride and to her modesty. This, I should imagine, must always be the case where she is not sure of a return to her attachment.

IN such a situation, to lay the heart open to any person whatever, does not appear to me consistent with the perfection of female delicacy. But perhaps I am in the wrong.—At the same time I must tell you, that, in point of prudence, it concerns you to attend well to the consequences of such a discovery. These secrets, however important in your own estimation, may appear very trifling to your friend, who possibly will not enter into your feelings, but may rather consider them as a subject of pleasantry. For this reason, love-secrets are of all others the worst kept. But the consequences to you may be very serious, as no man of spirit and delicacy ever valued a heart much hackneyed in the ways of love.

IF, therefore, you must have a friend to pour out your heart to, be sure of her honour and secrecy. Let her not be a married woman, especially if she lives happily with her husband, There are certain unguarded moments, in which such a woman, though the best and worthiest of her sex, may let hints escape, which at other times, or to any other person than her husband, she would be incapable of; nor will a husband in this case feel himself under the same obligation of secrecy and honour, as if you had put your confidence originally in himself, especially on a subject which the world is apt to treat so lightly.

IF all other circumstances are equal, there are obvious advantages in your making friends of one another. The ties of blood, and your being so much united in one common interest, form an additional bond of union to your friendship. If your brothers should have the good fortune to have hearts susceptible of friendship, to possess truth, honour, sense, and delicacy of sentiment, they are the fittest and most unexceptionable confidants. By placing confidence in them, you will receive every advantage which you could hope for from the friendship of men, without any of the inconveniencies that attend such connexions with our sex.

BEWARE of making confidants of your servants. Dignity not properly understood very readily degenerates into pride, which enters into no friendships, because it cannot bear an equal, and is so fond of flattery as to grasp at it even from servants and dependants. The most intimate confidants, therefore, of proud people are valets-de-chamber and waiting women. Shew the utmost humanity to your servants; make their situation as comfortable to them as is possible: but if you make them your confidants, you spoil them, and debase yourselves.

NEVER allow any person, under the pretended sanction of friendship, to be so familiar as to lose a proper respect for you. Never allow them to tease you on any subject that is disagreeable, or where you have once taken your resolution. Many will tell you, that this reserve is inconsistent with the freedom which friendship allows. But a certain respect is as necessary in friendship as in love. Without it, you may be liked as a child, but you will never be beloved as an equal.

THE temper and dispositions of the heart in your sex make you enter more readily and warmly into friendships than men. Your natural propensity to it is so strong, that you often run into intimacies which you soon have sufficient cause to repent of; and this makes your friendships so very fluctuating.

ANOTHER great obstacle to the sincerity as well as steadiness of your friendships is the great clashing of your interests in the pursuits of love, ambition, or vanity. For these reasons, it should appear at first view more eligible for you to contract your friendships with the men. Among other obvious advantages of an easy intercourse between the two sexes, it occasions an emulation and exertion in each to excel and be agreeable: hence their respective excellencies are mutually communicated and blended.—As their interests in no degree interfere, there can be no foundation for jealousy or suspicion of rivalship. The friendship of a man for a woman is always blended with a tenderness, which he never feels for one of his own sex, even where love is in no degree concerned. Besides we are conscious of a natural title you have to our protection and good offices, and therefore we feel an additional obligation of honour to serve you, and to observe an inviolable secrecy, whenever you confide in us.

BUT apply these observations with great caution. Thousands of women of the best hearts and finest parts have been ruined by men who approached them under the specious name of friendship. But supposing a man to have the most undoubted honour, yet his friendship to a woman is so near a-kin to love, that if she be very agreeable in her person, she will probably very soon find a lover, where she only wished to meet a friend. Let me here, however, warn you against that weakness so common among vain women, the imagination that every man who takes particular notice of you is a lover. Nothing can expose you more to ridicule, than the taking up a man on the suspicion of being your lover, who perhaps never once thought of you in that view, and giving yourselves those airs so common among silly women on such occasions.

THERE is a kind of unmeaning gallantry much practised by some men, which, if you have any discernment, you will find really harmless. Men of this sort will attend you to public places, and be useful to you by a number of little observances, which those of a superior class do not so well understand, or have not leisure to regard, or perhaps are too proud to submit to. Look on the compliments of such men as words of course, which they repeat to every agreeable woman of their acquaintance. There is a familiarity they are apt to assume, which a proper dignity in your behaviour will be easily able to check.

THERE is a different species of men whom you may like as agreeable companions, men of worth, taste and genius, whose conversation, in some respects, may be superior to what you generally meet with among your own sex. It will be foolish in you to deprive yourselves of an useful and agreeable acquaintance, merely because idle people say he is your lover. Such a man may like your company, without having any design on your person.

PEOPLE whose sentiments, and particularly whose tastes correspond, naturally like to associate together, although neither of them have the most distant view of any further connexion. But as this similarity of minds often gives rise to a more tender attachment than friendship, it will be prudent to keep a watchful eye over yourselves, lest your hearts become too far engaged before you are aware of it. At the same time, I do not think that your sex, at least in this part of the world, have much of that sensibility which disposes to such attachments. What is commonly called love among you is rather gratitude, and a partiality to the man who prefers you to the rest of your sex; and such a man you often marry, with little of either personal esteem or affection. Indeed, without an unusual share of natural sensibility, and very peculiar good fortune, a woman in this country has very little probability of marrying for love.

IT is a maxim laid down among you, and a very prudent one it is. That love is not to begin on your part, but is entirely to be the consequence of our attachment to you. Now, supposing a woman to have sense and taste, she will not find many men to whom she can possibly be supposed to bear any considerable share of esteem. Among these few, it is a very great chance if any of them distinguishes her particularly. Love, at least with us, is exceedingly capricious, and will not always fix where reason says it should. But supposing one of them should become particularly attached to her, it is still extremely improbable that he should be the man in the world her heart most approved of.

AS, therefore, Nature has not given you that unlimited range in your choice which we enjoy, she has wisely and benevolently assigned to you a greater flexibility of taste on this subject. Some agreeable qualities recommend a gentleman to your common good liking and friendship. In the course of his acquaintance, he contracts an attachment to you. When you perceive it, it excites your gratitude; this gratitude rises into a preference, and this preference perhaps at last advances to some degree of attachment, especially if it meets with crosses and difficulties, for these, and a state of suspense, are very great incitements to attachment, and are the food of love in both sexes. If attachment was not excited in your sex in this manner, there is not one of a million of you that could ever marry with any degree of love.

A MAN of taste and delicacy marries a woman because he loves her more than any other. A woman of equal taste and delicacy marries him because she esteems him, and because he gives her that preference. But if a man unfortunately becomes attached to a woman whose heart is secretly pre-engaged, his attachment, instead of obtaining a suitable return, is particularly offensive; and if he persists to teaze her, he makes himself equally the object of her scorn and aversion.

THE effects of love among men are diversified by their different tempers. An artful man may counterfeit every one of them so as easily to impose on a young girl of an open, generous, and feeling heart, if she is not extremely on her guard. The finest parts in such a girl may not always prove sufficient for her security. The dark and crooked paths of cunning are unsearchable, and inconceivable to an honourable and elevated mind.

THE following, I apprehend, are the most genuine effects of an honourable passion among the men, and the most difficult to counterfeit. A man of delicacy often betrays his passion by his too great anxiety to conceal it, especially if he has little hopes of success. True love, in all its stages, seeks concealment, and never expects success. It renders a man not only respectful, but timid to the highest degree in his behaviour to the woman he loves. To conceal the awe he stands in of her, he may sometimes affect pleasantry, but it sits aukwardly on him, and he quickly relapses into seriousness, if not into dulness. He magnifies all her real perfections in his imagination, and is either blind to her failings, or converts them into beauties. Like a person conscious of guilt, he is jealous that every eye observes him; and to avoid this, he shuns all the little observances of common gallantry.

HIS heart and his character will be improved in every respect by his attachment. His manners will become more gentle, and his conversation more agreeable; but diffidence and embarrassment will always make him appear to disadvantage in the company of his mistress. If the fascination continue long, it will totally depress his spirit, and extinguish every active, vigorous and manly principle of his mind. You will find this subject beautifully and pathetically painted in Thomson's Spring.

WHEN you observe in a gentleman's behaviour these marks which I have described above, reflect seriously what you are to do. If his attachment is agreeable to you, I leave you to do as nature, good sense, and delicacy shall direct you. If you love him let me advise you never to discover to him the full extent of your love, no not although you marry him. That sufficiently shews your preference, which is all he is entitled to know. If he has delicacy, he will ask for no stronger proof of your affection for your sake; if he has sense, he will not ask it for his own. This is an unpleasant truth, but it is my duty to let you know it; violent love cannot subsist, at least cannot be expressed, for any time together, on both sides; otherwise the certain consequence, however concealed, is satiety and disgust. Nature in this case has laid the reserve on you.

IF you see evident proofs of a gentleman's attachment, and are determined to shut your heart against him, as you ever hope to be used with generosity by the person who shall engage your own heart, treat him honourably and humanely. Do not let him linger in a miserable suspense, but be anxious to let him know your sentiments with regard to him.

HOWEVER people's hearts may deceive them, there is scarcely a person that can love for any time without at least some distant hope of success. If you really wish to undeceive a lover, you may do it in a variety of ways. There is a certain species of easy familiarity in your behaviour, which may satisfy him, if he has any discernment left, that he has nothing to hope for. But perhaps your particular temper may not admit of this.—You may easily shew that you want to avoid his company; but if he is a man whose friendship you wish to preserve, you may not chuse this method, because then you lose him in every capacity.—You may get a common friend to explain matters to him, or fall on many other devices, if you are seriously anxious to put him out of suspense.

BUT if you are resolved against every such method, at least do not shun opportunities of letting him explain himself. If you do this, you act barbarously and unjustly. If he brings you to an explanation, give him a polite, but resolute and decisive answer. In whatever way you convey your sentiments to him, if he is a man of spirit and delicacy, he will give you no further trouble, nor apply to your friends for their intercession. This last is a method of courtship which every man of spirit will disdain.—He will never whine nor sue for your pity. That would mortify him almost as much as your scorn. In short, you may possibly break such a heart, but you cannot bend it.—Great pride always accompanies delicacy, however concealed under the appearance of the utmost gentleness and modesty, and is the passion of all others the most difficult to conquer.

THERE is a case where a woman may coquette justifiably to the utmost verge which her conscience will allow. It is where a gentleman purposely declines to make his addresses, till such time as he thinks himself perfectly sure of her consent. This at bottom is intended to force a woman to give up the undoubted privilege of her sex, the privilege of her refusing; it is intended to force her to explain herself, in effect, before the gentleman deigns to do it, and by this mean to oblige her to violate the modesty and delicacy of her sex, and to invert the clearest order of nature. All this sacrifice is proposed to be made merely to gratify a most despicable vanity in a man who would degrade the very woman whom he wishes to make his wife.

IT is of great importance to distinguish, whether a gentleman who has the appearance of being your lover delays to speak explicitly, from the motive I have mentioned, or from a diffidence inseparable from true attachment. In the one case, you can scarcely use him too ill: in the other, you ought to use him with great kindness: and the greatest kindness you can shew him, if you are determined not to listen to his addresses, is to let him know it as soon as possible.

I KNOW the many excuses with which women endeavour to justify themselves to the world, and to their own consciences, when they act otherwise. Sometimes they plead ignorance, or at least uncertainty, of the gentleman's real sentiments. That may sometimes be the case. Sometimes they plead the decorums of their sex, which enjoin an equal behaviour to all men, and forbid them to consider any man as a lover, till he has directly told them so.—Perhaps few women carry their ideas of female delicacy and decorum so far as I do. But I must say, you are not entitled to plead the obligation of these virtues, in opposition to the superior ones of gratitude, justice, and humanity. The man is entitled to all these, who prefers you to the rest of your sex, and perhaps whose greatest weakness is this very preference. The truth of the matter is, vanity, and the love of admiration, are so prevailing passions among you, that you may be considered to make a very great sacrifice whenever you give up a lover, till every art of coquetry fails to keep him, or till he forces you to an explanation. You can be fond of the love, when you are indifferent to, or even when you despise the lover.

BUT the deepest and most artful coquetry is employed by women of superior taste and sense, to engage and fix the heart of a man whom the world and whom they themselves esteem, although they are firmly determined never to marry him. But his conversation amuses them, and his attachment is the highest gratification to their vanity; nay, they can sometimes be gratified with the utter ruin of his fortune, fame, and happiness.—God forbid I should ever think so of all your sex. I know many of them have principles, have generosity and dignity of soul that elevates them above the worthless vanity I have been speaking of.

SUCH a woman, I am persuaded, may always convert a lover, if she cannot give him her affections, into a warm and steady friend, provided he is a man of sense, resolution, and candour. If she explains herself to him with a generous openness and freedom, he must feel the stroke as a man; but he will likewise bear it as a man: what he suffers he will suffer in silence. Every sentiment of esteem will remain; but love though it requires very little food, and is easily surfeited with too much, yet it requires some. He will view her in the light of a married woman; and though passion subsides, yet a man of a candid and generous heart always retains a tenderness for a woman he has once loved, and who has used him well, beyond what he feels for any other of her sex.

IF he has not confided his own secret to any body, he has an undoubted title to ask you not to divulge it. If a woman chuses to trust any of her companions with her own unfortunate attachments, she may, as it is her own affair alone: but if she has any generosity or gratitude, she will not betray a secret which does not belong to her.

MALE coquetry is much more inexcusable than female, as well as more pernicious; but it is rare in this country. Very few men will give themselves the trouble to gain or retain any woman's affections, unless they have views on her either of an honourable or dishonourable kind. Men employed in the pursuits of business, ambition, or pleasure, will not give themselves the trouble to engage a woman's affections merely from the vanity of conquest, and of triumphing over the heart of an innocent and defenceless girl. Besides, people never value much what is entirely in their power. A man of parts, sentiment, and address, if he lays aside all regard to truth and humanity, may engage the hearts of fifty women at the same time, and may likewise conduct his coquetry with so much art, as to put it out of the power of any of them to specify a single expression that could be said to be directly expressive of love.

THIS ambiguity of behaviour, this art of keeping one in suspense, is the great secret of coquetry in both sexes. It is the more cruel in us, because we can carry it what length we please, and continue it as long as we please, without your being so much as at liberty to complain or expostulate; whereas we can break our chain, and force you to explain, whenever we become impatient of our situation.

I HAVE insisted the more particularly on this subject of courtship, because it may most readily happen to you at that early period of life when you can have little experience or knowledge of the world, when your passions are warm, and your judgments not arrived at such full maturity as to be able to correct them.—I wish you to possess such high principles of honour and generosity as will render you incapable of deceiving, and at the same time to possess that acute discernment which may secure you against being deceived.

A WOMAN, in this country, may easily prevent the first impressions of love, and every motive of prudence and delicacy should make her guard her heart against them, till such time as she has received the most convincing proof of the attachment of a man of such merit, as will justify a reciprocal regard. Your hearts indeed may be shut inflexibly and permanently against all the merit a man can possess. That may be your misfortune, but cannot be your fault. In such a situation, you would be equally unjust to yourself and your lover, if you gave him your hand when your heart revolted against him. But miserable will be your fate, if you allow an attachment to steal on you before you are sure of a return; or, what is infinitely worse, where there are wanting those qualities which alone can ensure happiness in a married state.

I KNOW nothing that renders a woman more despicable, than her thinking it essential to happiness to be married. Besides the gross indelicacy of the sentiment, it is a false one, as thousands of women have experienced. But if it was true, the belief that it is so, and the consequent impatience to be married, is the most effectual way to prevent it.

YOU must not think from this, that I do not wish you to marry. On the contrary, I am of opinion, that you may attain a superior degree of happiness in a married state, to what you can possibly find in any other. I know the forlorn and unprotected situation of an old maid, the chagrin and peevishness which are apt to infect their tempers, and the great difficulty of making a transition with dignity and chearfulness from the period of youth, beauty, admiration, and respect, into the calm, silent, unnoticed retreat of declining years.

I SEE some unmarried women of active, vigorous minds, and great vivacity of spirits, degrading themselves; sometimes by entering into a dissipated course of life, unsuitable to their years, and exposing themselves to the ridicule of girls, who might have been their grand-children; sometimes by oppressing their acquaintances by impertinent intrusions into their private affairs; and sometimes by being the propagators of scandal and defamation. All this is owing to an exuberant activity of spirit, which if it had found employment at home, would have rendered them respectable and useful members of society.

I SEE other women in the same situation, gentle, modest, blessed with sense, taste, delicacy, and every milder feminine virtue of the heart, but of weak spirits, bashful and timid: I see such women sinking into obscurity and insignificance, and gradually losing every elegant accomplishment; for this evident reason, that they are not united to a partner who has sense, and worth, and taste, to know their value; one who is able to draw forth their concealed qualities, and shew them to advantage; who can give that support to their feeble spirits which they stand so much in need of; and who, by his affection and tenderness, might make such a woman happy in exerting every talent, and accomplishing herself in every elegant art that could contribute to his amusement.

IN short, I am of opinion, that a married state, if entered into from proper motives of esteem and affection, will be the happiest for yourselves, and make you most respectable in the eyes of the world, and the most useful members of society. But I confess I am not enough of a patriot to wish you to marry for the good of the public. I wish you to marry for no other reason but to make yourselves happier. When I am so particular in my advices about your conduct, I own my heart beats with the fond hope of making you worthy the attachment of men who will deserve you, and be sensible of your merit. But heaven forbid you should ever relinquish the ease and independence of a single life, to become the slaves of a fool, or a tyrant's caprice.

AS these have been always my sentiments, I shall do you but justice, when I leave you in such independent circumstances as may lay you under no temptation to do from necessity what you would never do from choice.—This will likewise save you from that cruel mortification to a woman of spirit, the suspicion that a gentleman thinks he does you an honour or a favour when he asks you for his wife.

IF I live till you arrive at that age when you shall be capable to judge for yourselves, and do not strangely alter my sentiments, I shall act towards you in a very different manner from what most parents do. My opinion has always been, that when that period arrives, the parental authority ceases.

I HOPE I shall always treat you with that affection and easy confidence which may dispose you to look on me as your friend. In that capacity alone I shall think myself entitled to give you my opinion; in the doing of which, I should think myself highly criminal, if I did not to the utmost of my power endeavour to divest myself of all personal vanity, and all prejudices in favour of my particular taste. If you did not chuse to follow my advice, I should not on that account cease to love you as my children.—Though my right to your obedience was expired, yet I should think nothing could release me from the ties of nature and humanity.

YOU may perhaps imagine, that the reserved behaviour which I recommend to you, and your appearing seldom at public places, must cut off all opportunities of your being acquainted with gentlemen. I am very far from intending this. I advise you to no reserve, but what will render you more respected and beloved by our sex. I do not think public places suited to make people acquainted together. They can only be distinguished there by their looks and external behaviour. But it is in private companies alone where you can expect easy and agreeable conversation, which I should never wish you to decline. If you do not allow gentlemen to become acquainted with you, you can never expect to marry with attachment on either side.—Love is very seldom produced at first sight; at least it must have, in that case, a very unjustifiable foundation. True love is founded on esteem, in a correspondence of tastes and sentiments, and steals on the heart imperceptibly.

THERE is one advice I shall leave you, to which I beg your particular attention: Before your affections come to be in the least engaged to any man, examine your tempers, your tastes, and your hearts, very severely, and settle in your own minds, what are the requisites to your happiness in a married state; and as it is almost impossible that you should get every thing you wish, come to a steady determination what you are to consider as essential, and what may be sacrificed.

IF you have hearts disposed by nature for love and friendship, and possess those feelings which enable you to enter into all the refinements and delicacies of these attachments, consider well, for heaven's sake, and as you value your future happiness, before you give them any indulgence. If you have the misfortune (for a very great misfortune it commonly is to your sex) to have such a temper and such sentiments deeply rooted in you, if you have spirit and resolution to resist the solicitations of vanity, the persecution of friends (for you will have lost the only friend that would never persecute you) and can support the prospect of the many inconveniencies attending the state of an old maid, which I formerly pointed out, then you may indulge yourselves in that kind of sentimental reading and conversation which is most correspondent to your feelings.

BUT if you find, on a strict self-examination, that marriage is absolutely essential to your happiness, keep the secret inviolable in your own bosoms, for the reason I formerly mentioned; but shun as you would do the most fatal poison, all that species of reading and conversation which warms the imagination, which engages and softens the heart, and raises the taste above the level of common life. If you do otherwise, consider the terrible conflict of passions this may afterwards raise in your breasts.

IF this refinement once takes deep root in your minds, and you do not obey its dictates, but marry from vulgar and mercenary views, you may never be able to eradicate it entirely, and then it will imbitter all your married days. Instead of meeting with sense, delicacy, tenderness, a lover, a friend, an equal companion, in a husband, you may be tired with insipidity and dullness; shocked with indelicacy, or mortified by indifference. You will find none to compassionate, or even understand your sufferings; for your husbands may not use you cruelly, and may give you as much money for your clothes, personal expense, and domestic necessaries, as is suitable to their fortunes. The world therefore would look on you as unreasonable women, and that did not deserve to be happy, if you were not so.—To avoid these complicated evils, if you are determined at all events to marry, I would advise you to make all your reading and amusements of such a kind, as do not affect the heart nor the imagination, except in the way of wit or humour.

I HAVE no view by these advices to lead your tastes; I only want to persuade you of the necessity of knowing your own minds, which, though seemingly very easy, is what your sex seldom attain on many important occasions in life, but particularly on this of which I am speaking. There is not a quality I more anxiously wish you to possess, than that collected decisive spirit which rests on itself, which enables you to see where your true happiness lies, and to pursue it with the most determined resolution. In matters of business, follow the advice of those who know them better than yourselves, and in whose integrity you can confide; but in matters of taste, that depend on your own feelings, consult no one friend whatever, but consult your own hearts.

IF a gentleman makes his addresses to you, or gives you reason to believe he will do so, before you allow your affections to be engaged, endeavour in the most prudent and secret manner, to procure from your friends every necessary piece of information concerning him; such as his character for sense, his morals, his temper, fortune and family; whether it is distinguished for parts and worth, or for folly, knavery, and loathsome hereditary diseases. When your friends inform you of these, they have fulfilled their duty. If they go further, they have not that deference for you which a becoming dignity on your part would effectually command.

WHATEVER your views are in marrying, take every possible precaution to prevent their being disappointed. If fortune, and the pleasures it brings, are your aim, it is not sufficient that the settlements of a jointure and children's provisions be ample, and properly secured; it is necessary that you should enjoy the fortune during your own life. The principal security you can have for this will depend on your marrying a good-natured generous man, who despises money, and who will let you live where you can best enjoy that pleasure, that pomp and parade of life for which you married him.

FROM what I have said, you will easily see that I could never pretend to advise whom you should marry; but I can with great confidence advise whom you should not marry.

AVOID a companion that may entail any hereditary disease on your posterity, particularly (that most dreadful of all human calamities) madness. It is the height of imprudence to run into such a danger, and in my opinion, highly criminal.

Do not marry a fool; he is the most intractable of all animals; he is led by his passions and caprices, and is incapable of hearing the voice of reason. It may probably too hurt your vanity to have husbands for whom you have reason to blush and tremble every time they open their lips in company. But the worst circumstance, that attends a fool, is his constant jealousy of his wife being thought to govern him. This renders it impossible to lead him, and he is continually doing absurd and disagreeable things, for no other reason but to shew he dares do them.

A RAKE is always a suspicious husband, because he has only known the most worthless of your sex. He likewise entails the worst diseases on his wife and children, if he has the misfortune to have any.

IF you have a sense of religion yourselves, do not think of husbands who have none. If they have tolerable understandings, they will be glad that you have religion, for their own sakes, and for the sake of their families; but it will sink you in their esteem. If they are weak men, they will be continually teazing and shocking you about your principles.—If you have children, you will suffer the most bitter distress, in seeing all your endeavours to form their minds to virtue and piety, all your endeavours to secure their present and eternal happiness frustrated, and turned into ridicule.

AS I look on your choice of a husband to be of the greatest consequence to your happiness, I hope you will make it with the utmost circumspection. Do not give way to a sudden sally of passion, and dignify it with the name of love.—Genuine love is not founded in caprice; it is founded in nature, on honourable views, on virtue, on similarity of tastes and sympathy of souls.

IF you have these sentiments, you will never marry any one, when you are not in that situation, in point of fortune, which is necessary to the happiness of either of you. What that competency may be, can only be determined by your own tastes. It would be ungenerous in you to take advantage of a lover's attachment, to plunge him into distress; and if he has any honour, no personal gratification will ever tempt him to enter into any connection which will render you unhappy. If you have as much between you as to satisfy all your reasonable demands, it is sufficient.

I SHALL conclude with endeavouring to remove a difficulty which must naturally occur to any woman of reflection on the subject of marriage. What is to become of all these refinements of delicacy, that dignity of manners, which checked all familiarities, and suspended desire in respectful and awful admiration? In answer to this, I shall only observe, that if motives of interest or vanity have had any share in your resolutions to marry, none of these chimerical notions will give you any pain; nay they will very quickly appear as ridiculous in your own eyes, as they probably always did in the eyes of your husbands. They have been sentiments which have floated in your imaginations, but have never reached your hearts. But if these sentiments have been truly genuine, and if you have had the singular happy fate to attach those who understand them, you have no reason to be afraid.

MARRIAGE indeed, will at once dispel the enchantment raised by external beauty; but the virtues and graces that first warmed the heart, that reserve and delicacy which always left the lover something further to wish, and often made him doubtful of your sensibility or attachment, may and ought ever to remain. The tumult of passion will necessarily subside; but it will be succeeded by an endearment, that affects the heart in a more equal, more sensible, and tender manner.—But I must check myself, and not indulge in descriptions that may mislead you, and that too sensibly awake the remembrance of my happier days, which, perhaps, it were better for me to forget forever.

I HAVE thus given you my opinion on some of the most important articles of your future life, chiefly calculated for that period when you are just entering the world. I have endeavoured to avoid some peculiarities of opinion, which, from their contradiction to the general practice of the world, I might reasonably have suspected were not so well founded. But in writing to you, I am afraid my heart has been too full, and too warmly interested, to allow me to keep this resolution. This may have produced some embarrassment, and some seeming contradictions. What I have written has been the amusement of some solitary hours, and has served to divert some melancholy reflections.—I am conscious I undertook a task to which I was very unequal; but I have discharged a part of my duty.—You will at least be pleased with it, as the last mark of your father's love and attention.

THE END.

Milton Keynes UK
Ingram Content Group UK Ltd.
UKHW030626061024
449204UK00004B/284